'The role of design-led thinking has become essential to how we grow and thrive as organisations and nations. As one of Australia's foremost Design Thinking, innovation and experimentation experts, Nathan shares his tips, tricks, methods and learnings for successfully mastering the innovation process. *Innovator's Playbook* is a must-have for any organisation looking to put innovation first.'

Rear Admiral Wendy Malcolm, Royal Australian Navy, Head of Maritime Systems, Capability Acquisition and Sustainment Group

'Every business I come across wants to be more innovative. The challenge I hear time and time again is, 'we know we need to do this but we don't know where to start'. *Innovator's Playbook* is a brilliant book that links the process of creativity, design and innovation to business success in a practical, tangible and easy to digest manner. At a time when our world is facing ever-increasing complexity, this is a must read for every business leader.'

Dr Brandon Gien, CEO Good Design Australia. President Emeritus, World Design Organization.

'"… most innovations fail because of little or poor work at the front end of innovation." I couldn't agree more, but in order to solve for this, you need your team to be trained for it. Nathan has a unique ability to put people at ease, explain pretty complex topics in digestible chunks and get everyone stuck in and trying out new skills.'

Inga Latham, Chief Product Officer, Siteminder

'One of the most practical books on innovation I have ever read. A fantastic tool for both the biggest and smallest of businesses.'

Rob Weston, former Global Brand and Marketing Director, Marks & Spencer

T0357918

'It's only appropriate that Nathan Baird has written the playbook on innovation. Nathan has helped dozens of companies of all sizes solve customer problems by creating new and innovative solutions which stand the test of time by being desirable, feasible and viable. *Innovator's Playbook* is an essential guide for anyone wanting to succeed in an increasingly crowded market of new ideas.'

Albert Naffah, General Manager Payments Development & Strategy, Commonwealth Bank of Australia

NATHAN BAIRD

HOW TO
CREATE GREAT
PRODUCTS,
SERVICES
& EXPERIENCES

INNOVATOR'S
PLAYBOOK

THAT YOUR
CUSTOMERS
WILL LOVE!

WILEY

First published in 2020 by John Wiley & Sons Australia, Ltd
42 McDougall St, Milton Qld 4064

Office also in Melbourne

Typeset in Overpass Light 11pt/14pt

© John Wiley & Sons Australia, Ltd 2020

The moral rights of the author have been asserted

ISBN: 978-0-730-38364-2

NATIONAL LIBRARY OF AUSTRALIA

A catalogue record for this book is available from the National Library of Australia

All rights reserved. Except as permitted under the *Australian Copyright Act 1968* (for example, a fair dealing for the purposes of study, research, criticism or review), no part of this book may be reproduced, stored in a retrieval system, communicated or transmitted in any form or by any means without prior written permission. All inquiries should be made to the publisher at the address above.

Cover, matter and stage opener design by Kyely Williams, Gamut Design

Some figures use images from: © advent/Shutterstock, © VLADGRIN/ Getty Images, © Mosquito-/iStockphoto, © artsstock/Getty Images, © Giraphics/Shutterstock, © chris scredon/iStockphoto, © alphaspirit/ Getty Images, © dizain/Shutterstock, multiple images by Pixaline from Pixabay, image by Pixel_perfect from Pixabay, image by Devanath from Pixabay, image by Clker-Free-Vector-Images from Pixabay, image by TukTukDesign from Pixabay, image by Pettycon from Pixabay, image by 200 Degrees from Pixabay, image by Megan Rexazin from Pixabay, image by gdakaska from Pixabay, image by OpenClipart-Vectors from Pixabay

Printed in Singapore by Markono Print Media Pte Ltd

10 9 8 7 6 5 4 3 2 1

Disclaimer

The material in this publication is of the nature of general comment only, and does not represent professional advice. It is not intended to provide specific guidance for particular circumstances and it should not be relied on as the basis for any decision to take action or not take action on any matter which it covers. Readers should obtain professional advice where appropriate, before making any such decision. To the maximum extent permitted by law, the author and publisher disclaim all responsibility and liability to any person, arising directly or indirectly from any person taking or not taking action based on the information in this publication.

CONTENTS

MY JOURNEY OF DISCOVERY TO INNOVATION FLOW

Innovation is one of the riskiest,
yet most important,
endeavours of modern times.

We've all heard about the need for innovation and its importance in organisations and economies. We know its value. In organisations innovation drives growth. For example, Procter & Gamble Chairman and CEO (and co-author of *The Game Changer*) A. G. Lafley used innovation to turn the P&G business around and create 'sustained and ever-improving organic revenue growth and profits', choosing innovation as the key driver because it is 'the best way to win in this world'.

For humankind innovation drives development and helps us reach fulfilment. The human race has developed through creativity and innovation. In his best-selling book *Flow*, Professor Mihaly Csikszentmihalyi shares how, when we are involved in creativity and innovation, 'we feel that we are living more fully than during the rest of life'.

Ultimately, organisations, the people within them, and the whole population, in fact, need the ability to innovate in order to develop, grow and reach any kind of fulfilment. Without it we'll all stagnate and possibly not even survive.

Yet innovation is hard and rarely successful. According to Harvard Business School professor Clayton Christensen 95 per cent of new products fail. And 'most start-ups fail', says start-up guru and author of the *Lean Startup*, Eric Ries. So, just like we need to continually innovate to grow and develop, we also need to continually grow and develop how we innovate.

What do we mean by 'innovation'? I see innovation as the act of challenging the status quo to create new value that satisfies a human need.

If we break this down, then we are saying that innovation:

> » is a verb; it is something you do

> » challenges the status quo: think Cirque du Soleil, Apple's iPod and iPhone, Nespresso, Uber, Airbnb

> » must create new value; if it doesn't, then it is just creativity (or fun) without action and less likely to be successful

» must satisfy a human need; there is a human need at the end (or beginning) of every innovation. These humans can be customers, consumers, citizens, employees, end users and so on. For simplicity, throughout the remainder of this book I refer to all these types of humans as 'customers'. The methods and lessons in this book are equally applicable to innovating for any one of these groups.

When we think of innovation we may think of new products, experiences, services or better ways of working (e.g. new systems and processes). The broad range of innovation is well illustrated by figure 1, global innovation firm Doblin's Ten Types of Innovation.

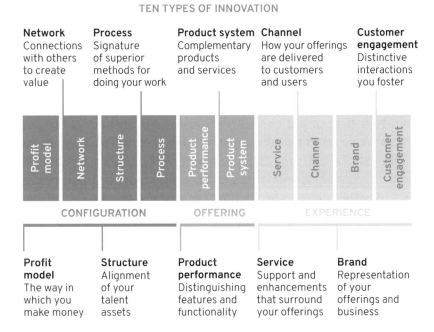

Figure 1: Doblin's Ten Types of Innovation
Source: Larry Keeley, Ryan Pikkel, Brian Quinn and Helen Walters, *Ten Types of Innovation: The Discipline of Building Breakthroughs* (Hoboken, New Jersey: John Wiley & Sons, 2013)

MY JOURNEY

After graduating with a Masters in Commerce—my thesis was on branding—I started out as a sales representative for FMCG (fast-moving consumer goods) giant Unilever. This was a great place for me to start my career, and all part of my plan of becoming a brand manager. In my final years studying Marketing at university many of the examples of great branding came from the FMCG industry; I was hooked and wanted to become a brand manager on an iconic FMCG brand—think Coca-Cola, Gillette, Guinness, and so on. The advice given to me by those who'd already 'made it' was to start out at the coalface in sales before moving into brand management.

After four years at several divisions of Unilever in New Zealand and the UK, managing various brands, I had a bit of a personal reckoning; Unilever was a great consumer-centric organisation, but I realised I was only getting to do the stuff I loved (strategic brand work and new product innovation) on average one day a fortnight. I wasn't unleashing my creativity enough, and, as Csikszentmihalyi would say, I wasn't in 'flow'—and, frankly, it was contributing to making me very depressed. I looked at what I had enjoyed about my previous roles and what was missing and decided I wanted to work as a brand and innovation consultant for a brand consultancy, and I haven't looked back.

I loved that first brand consultancy role. I got to help clients and their teams develop new brand strategies, reposition their brands and innovate new products and services. I got to do the things I loved to do as a brand manager and account manager, but on a daily basis and without all the project management and administration.

If we were to take the key learnings from this experience, I'd say they were that I stopped and reflected on my feelings and distilled these into needs before jumping to solution or a new job. I then 'prototyped and tested' these possible new jobs by spending a few days working at a couple of agencies and brand consultancies before pursuing one of these roles.

I've since spent the last 17 years helping organisations and teams grow and be more fulfilled through brand strategy and innovation. Over this time I've continually learned, experimented and refined techniques around the question: when does innovation succeed and fail, and what is a method for repeatable success that we can all apply?

My studies and then roles at Unilever really piqued my interest in how organisations and teams could repeatedly innovate more successfully, whether that be for new products, experiences and services or better ways of working, such as internal systems and processes. I'd had some success at Unilever with the experienced people I worked with and the excellent processes Unilever had in place, but I knew organisations and teams could still improve further.

There were many books on building a culture of innovation, which, while important, weren't about the process of innovation. One book on this topic that did really stand out was Robert G. Cooper's *Winning at New Products*. Firstly, it stood out because it drew on a number of studies from the field, looking at what separated the winners from the losers in product innovation; it was rich with research results. Secondly, it related this to the Stage Gate Innovation process that almost all leading FMCG companies, including Unilever, were using at the time.

The most significant finding in Cooper's work in my view was that most innovations fail because of little or poor work at the front end of innovation. The 'front end' of innovation being the stages from project initiation, exploratory research, customer need generation, ideation to concept development (prototyping and testing). Everything that comes before development, commercialisation and launch. The number one factor was poor customer research – 'a lack of thoroughness in identifying real needs in the marketplace', with innovation teams often 'making assumptions in order to justify the project'. Quality work was often missing, and very few resources were being allocated to these early stages: 'Only 7% of the money and 16% of the work effort (person-days) goes to the vital pre-development (front-end) phases of the project!' The time pressures to launch are the main drivers of skipping or doing these stages poorly. Speed in innovation is very important, but not at the expense of managing the innovation journey properly. In fact, it is often a false economy, with this rushing of stages resulting in rework or project failure in the middle and back end of the process. The further you progress along the innovation journey, the more time- and resource-intensive and expensive it becomes. So getting your upfront work done right is critical; it lays the foundation for everything that follows.

While it is important to fix these weaknesses, Cooper also wanted to identify what the winning strategies were. To answer this research question Cooper investigated 2000 product innovation projects—two thirds were successes and one third were failures. From these case studies he identified nine success factors:

1. a unique, superior and differentiated product with good value-for-money for the customer

2. a strong market orientation—voice of customer built in

3. a sharp, early, fact-based product definition before development begins

4. solid up-front homework—doing the front-end activities well

5. true cross-functional teams—empowered, resourced, accountable, dedicated leader

6. leverage—where the product builds on the business's technology and marketing competencies

7. market attractiveness—size, growth, margins

8. quality of the launch effort—well planned, properly resourced

9. technological competencies and quality of execution of technological activities.

As you can see, five of the nine success factors are related to the front end of the innovation process, with a further two being equally attributable to both the front and back end. Of the five directly attributable to the front end, according to Cooper's research the first four have the biggest effect on success overall.

It was pretty clear to my young self that if we could improve the front end of innovation we would dramatically improve its success. While the back end could still be improved, it was already far stronger and this wasn't where my passion or skills lay. This gap gave me purpose; I wanted to build on the significant contributions by the likes of Cooper and organisations such as Unilever. I was passionate and I was curious, so I focused on researching what others had found and then practically applying it in the field on real projects, generating and applying my own thinking, working with colleagues and clients—experimenting with it all and keeping what worked and filing what didn't.

17 YEARS LATER ...

Innovation is still very difficult, and success rates don't appear to be improving. Why is this?

Over this time I've been lucky enough to work with some of the most innovative and successful organisations, and those with ambitions to be (as well as those who were at the peak of their performance only to be disrupted by a new player), such as Air New Zealand, The Australian Institute of Sport, Bausch & Lomb, Cadbury, Coca-Cola, Diageo, Commonwealth Bank, Kraft, Les Mills, Mondelez, Nestlé, Nokia (in its heyday), Sainsbury's, Siemens ...

And it is this journey that has led me to writing this book. To share with you my learnings and experiences of what works and what doesn't.

This is not a book of scientifically researched methods — that hasn't been the journey I chose. It is practical and applied. It is based on tens of thousands of hours leading and training innovation, thousands of workshops and hundreds of client partnerships and collaborations across multiple industries and continents. It is a story, and method, of what works from experience.

Learnings

- Most innovations fail because of too little or poor work at the front end of the innovation process.

- The biggest culprit is poor customer research; that is, a lack of rigour in identifying real unmet customer needs and validating the solutions through real customer testing.

WHAT'S ALL THIS NOISE ABOUT DESIGN?

Design is the 'in' word — but what does it mean? And should you care?

The word 'design' has become a substitute for what we called 'insight-led innovation' when I was starting my career at Unilever. (And it was probably a substitute for an even earlier term before that!)

I cut my teeth on product innovation or new product development (NPD) in the FMCG industry. Back then design was a specialist field that mostly required a tertiary qualification and creativity of the creative arts type. Designers were graphic and brand, or product or industrial designers. While any marketing or innovation team worth its salt would involve designers early in the process of brand development and innovation, their role pretty much was to apply their creativity and design skills to bring the ideas to life in the concept phase for testing, and then to design the final solution. This was design as form, function and styling. For example, if you were developing a new beer to launch, the bottle design would be done by the industrial or product designer and the graphics for the brand, label and packaging would be designed by the graphic designer.

Here is an example of the front end of our NPD process from back then. These were the key steps post innovation strategy and prior to business case, development and launch:

1. Project Initiation
2. Customer Research
3. Insight Generation
4. Idea Generation
5. Concept Development
6. Concept Research
7. Product, Packaging and Brand Development briefs.

If you are already familiar with Design Thinking (and its different guises, such as Human Centred Design and Customer Centric Design) you'll recognise the similarity in the processes. In fact, apart from a few new or evolved tools, the steps are exactly the same. Just replace some of the words, e.g. 'customer research' with 'empathise', 'concept' with 'prototype' and 'concept research' with 'test'. So why is Design Thinking seen as this great new methodology when it is merely a new name for something that has existed, at least in some industries such as FMCG, for a long time?

First of all it's because, while it may have been mainstream in FMCG, it wasn't in other industries. So why was that? The FMCG industry, with the likes of Procter & Gamble (P&G) and Unilever, created the practice of building products into brands and moving from being manufacturing led to marketing led. Marketing done well in FMCG was always about being customer or consumer centric, which is the central pillar of Design Thinking. Continuous innovation and the development and launch of new products each season or year was (and still is) central to the prosperity of FMCG companies. In the early 2000s retail power was increasing, consumers were becoming more demanding and sophisticated, and media and markets were fragmenting. The two most successful ways to counter these threats were by building strong brands and innovating new products. Many other industries, including the service sector, weren't so marketing- or customer-centric. They focused on service, but not the higher order experience design.

And then there were the designers themselves. They were involved in the innovation process to apply design to the specific stages relevant to their skills, for example concept design and final product design. They were using many of the elements of Design Thinking, but were not responsible for or oversaw the full process, for example elements such as the upfront strategy, customer research and marketing. It wasn't until product design companies such as IDEO started moving upstream into strategy and research and broadening their offering that the term 'Design Thinking' got coined. And I believe IDEO openly acknowledge that it is a new term for something that has existed for a long time, albeit only in some industries. So prior to this the likes of IDEO were predominantly still product design consultancies and the Institute of Design at Stanford (d.school), a famed hub for evangelising and popularising Design Thinking, didn't even exist.

So we've seen design evolve from styling, form and function to design as a *process*—and it hasn't stopped there.

DESIGN TAKES OVER

So 'design' started to represent the entire innovation journey: not only the design of better products, services or experiences, but also better systems, processes and even business strategy and business models. Design was increasingly becoming the means for innovation—to such an extent that in the last decade 'design' has become the verb and 'innovation' the noun. Design is starting to get a seat at the upper management table, with some organisations now having a Chief Design Officer. This evolution or journey is well illustrated by the Extended Danish Design Ladder. I was first exposed to it by Professor Sam Bucolo, who was heading up University of Technology Sydney's Design and Innovation Research Centre, which I was partnering with on some projects. In his book *Are We There Yet?*, Sam explains how the ladder was developed by the Danish Design Centre in 2003 'as a tool to measure the level of design activity in businesses'. While the original Danish Design Ladder stops at 'design as a business strategy', Sam has adapted it by adding two more steps: 'design as organisational transformation' and 'design as a national competitive strategy' (see figure 2). From my observations most organisations and industries are in the stage of moving from step 2, 'design as styling', to step 3, 'design as an innovation process'. And of course there are still many at the bottom rung of the ladder, at 'non-design'. But, while there is still so much potential for design in business, industry and society as a whole, my focus in this book is to help organisations first master design as an innovation process for creating new products, services, experiences and better ways of working. From experience once this is mastered it can then be applied progressively up the ladder to strategy, transformation and economic development.

Design as a process, or 'Design Thinking', borrows from and builds on many older fields and disciplines to encapsulate an integrated approach to innovation from:

» strategy to determine where to play and how to win

» qualitative research to observe and interview customers to identify what is important to them and then distill these into needs and insights

- » innovation and brand facilitation to generate ideas and facilitate workshops
- » traditional designers to prototype and qualitative research again to test these prototypes with customers
- » business strategy to develop the business models for realising these prototypes and making them feasible and viable.

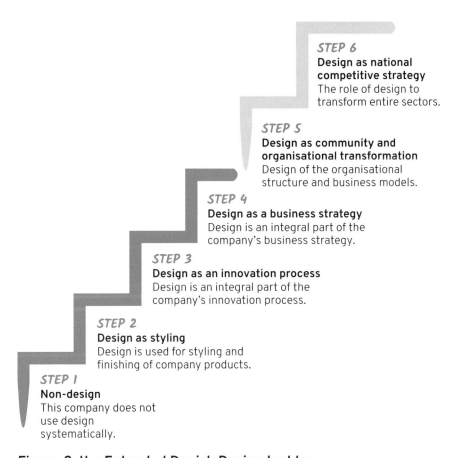

STEP 6
Design as national competitive strategy
The role of design to transform entire sectors.

STEP 5
Design as community and organisational transformation
Design of the organisational structure and business models.

STEP 4
Design as a business strategy
Design is an integral part of the company's business strategy.

STEP 3
Design as an innovation process
Design is an integral part of the company's innovation process.

STEP 2
Design as styling
Design is used for styling and finishing of company products.

STEP 1
Non-design
This company does not use design systematically.

Figure 2: the Extended Danish Design Ladder
Source: Sam Bucolo, *Are We There Yet?*, BIS Publishers, 2016

Good design and innovation requires strategic thinking, curiosity, empathy, insightfulness, creativity, experimentation and business acumen plus much more! But a Design Thinker alone cannot do all of this themselves. I'm a passionate Design Thinking advocate, but I always stress to the teams I'm working with that there is a difference between being trained in Design Thinking and being a specialist in each of the stages and the tools. I still prefer (and encourage you) to engage researchers, designers, developers, financial analysts and other specialists and experts to play their roles. Success in innovation requires you to work with a cross-functional team and work alongside and learn from other functional and subject matter experts. So while Design Thinking has borrowed from the designer's toolbox, it has also borrowed from the strategists, researchers, innovators, facilitators, FMCG marketers and many others.

Innovation is a team sport and no one person, role or industry field can do or own the entire innovation (design) journey. None of us can be a deep expert at every stage of the innovation journey, or as good as a high-performing collaborative team of specialists. A good Design Thinker is a T-shaped person who understands the entire innovation journey and is a deep expert with specialisation in one or two of the phases, for example insight generation or ideation or facilitation. (The horizontal bar of the 'T' represents their ability to understand the entire innovation journey and collaborate across disciplines with experts in other areas, and the vertical bar represents their deep expertise and specialisation in one or more of the disciplines.)

So design beyond styling, as an innovation process, is new to more industries than not. And while in recent times it has become well known and its use is now fairly widespread I would argue from experience that its practice and use is still fairly immature.

In addition to Design Thinking, in recent years there has been an influx of new, reinvented and adapted 'design' methodologies to help us be more successful at innovation and entrepreneurship: Business Model Thinking, Lean Startup, Lean Manufacturing and Agile (although this is more a development and project management methodology). Design Thinking and Business Model Thinking are predominantly front end of innovation methods. Agile and Lean Manufacturing are predominantly back-end methods, with Lean Startup being the glue between front and back.

JUMPING TO SOLUTIONS

For all of these new methodologies, innovation is still very difficult and success rates don't appear to be improving. Why is this? And how can we use these methodologies better to increase our innovation success rates?

For one, we're still not getting the front end of innovation right. 'Why?', you ask. One of the biggest problems is a compulsion to jump to the solution and start building a new product or service too soon. What's so wrong about jumping to the solution and starting building? After all, surely this leads to getting to market faster. Well, as we know from the previous section, it doesn't actually get you to market quicker. Jumping to the solution results in more defects, more rework and more costly failures overall. Spending time and money up front decreases these defects and ensures you build a superior, unique and relevant new product – the number one driver of innovation success, according to Robert Cooper. As the old adage says, 'a stitch in time saves nine': putting the time in early ultimately helps you get to market quicker. Furthermore, by jumping to the solution you are not innovating based on an identified customer need (the number one reason innovations fail, according to Cooper) and, secondly, you are going to narrow too soon. So if your solution fails in concept testing (and it's likely to, because you haven't identified an important and unmet customer need) you are left with nowhere to go except back to the drawing board and more jumping to the solution. And so the continuous cycle of pivoting and re-pivoting occurs: solution – test – fail – solution – test – fail.

Now, don't get me wrong: if you think you have identified a great idea that meets a market need, then go and test it, by all means. But if you want to increase your chances at success or are trying to build a repeatable and successful approach to innovation, then start with the customer, or, as Ash Maurya, author of both *Running Lean* and *Scaling Lean* says, 'fall in love with the problem, not the solution'. Needs are enduring; solutions and technologies come and go over time. In **stage 2: Discover** I'll detail how a customer-centric approach is actually not only more effective, but also faster.

WHY DO THEY JUMP?

So what is driving this behaviour of jumping to the solution? From my experience it is two things:

1. time pressure
2. human nature.

First is the constant pressure from senior management for their teams to get on with building and launching their solutions more quickly. These senior leaders are driven by the market's obsession for short-term results, and often they are willing to take short-cuts in the early stages to see tangible progress. Understandably, they are also more comfortable in the more predictable and measurable build and launch stages of a project versus the less predictable, uncertain, complex and ambiguous front-end stages of searching for unmet needs and creating and experimenting with solutions to meet these needs. Some of these senior managers have been promoted for successfully growing existing product lines and businesses in a time, where success could be achieved through more traditional and predictable methods. However, in today's fast-changing world of globalisation, maturing categories, technological advances and disruption, to name but a few trends, the ability to manage in a VUCA (volatile, uncertain, complex and ambiguous) world and to innovate is going to be a prerequisite for all leaders.

Secondly, from my experience it would appear to be human nature to want to jump to the solution. Most of us love the idea generation stage of projects, and it's something we can all participate in — we can all have ideas. Yet fewer of us are good at the customer research, synthesis and generating insights that should occur beforehand. If you take this human element piece and couple it with keen, but inexperienced practitioners joining the fervent following of these new 'design' methods, then you risk a mass movement of jumping to the solution and skipping the critical front end of innovation. The mass adoption of better ways to innovate and design is great for the private and public sectors and the world as a whole, but unfortunately, sometimes the confidence and ambitions of new practitioners are running ahead of their skills. John Kembel, one of Stanford d.school's co-founders, likens it to the beginner skiers you see on the ski slopes; they cause mayhem and injury on the mountain because their ambition and confidence runs ahead of their skills. Now, we've all been there, and speaking from experience I know my own skills improve a lot more quickly and safely under the tutelage of an experienced instructor, and a two-day training course in skiing or snowboarding isn't enough to get you to mastery (or black runs).

It takes time to get the battle scars and learn the rigour that can only come from the experience of running multiple design and innovation projects and failing on a few. Budding Design Thinkers can reel off all the buzz words and some can even put on an impressive performance, but as soon as the innovation project leaves the boot-camp curriculum (off piste, so to speak), as innovation projects so often do, they struggle and fail to deliver on the expectations of those impatient leaders who feel safe with predictability. The bigger impact of all of this is that those senior stakeholders (not to mention the required collaborators from other departments), who were already a bit suspicious and cynical of these methods, see it as another fluffy and fruitless exercise in customer emotions, butcher paper and sticky notes. In the short term the project gets shut down, but in the longer term the methodology and a customer-centric design-led approach to innovation and business gets culled. These passionate enthusiasts need the next level of detail: a rigorous framework, tools, skills, mindsets and 'how to's' that take them beyond the boot camp!

Innovator's Playbook

INTEGRATING THE NEW DESIGN METHODS TO IMPROVE INNOVATION SUCCESS RATES

When there is a failure to deliver results, on top of an at-times fanatical obsession for these new methods, then they can get a bad rap. In my experience these new methodologies have proven to help us innovate better, but only if they are used in the right way, at the right time, and integrated in the right sequence. However, I see too many authors, advisers, consultants, innovation teams and organisations using these methods in the wrong way, at the wrong time, and in many cases to support their own compulsion or agenda to jump to the solution without doing the important customer discovery and insight generation work first. Written about, taught or facilitated in the wrong way, many of these tools are actually encouraging this epidemic of jumping to the solution and failure!

To help us better understand how to use these methods in the right way to master the front end of innovation it is useful to first quickly understand some of the misuses so you can avoid these traps and pitfalls.

DESIGN THINKING

Let's start with Design Thinking. Design Thinking is a human-centred, creative and experimentation-driven approach to innovation and transformation. First of all let's acknowledge that Design Thinking has done a lot for the field of innovation and design; it has given fresh emphasis and impetus to this field. It has driven awareness, and democratised and mainstreamed innovation for the masses. Design Thinking forms the base for my approach and I've been using it for 19 years, since before it was even called Design Thinking.

It's not surprising that a method this popular gets mixed results depending on who's using it and their level of experience. But where I see Design Thinking going especially wrong is beginners doing the empathy stage (research) themselves rather than engaging specialist researchers to at least guide and lead them. This is something people are trained to do and spend their entire profession doing. You can't gain that experience and expertise in a two-day boot camp. And then, 'define', or the insight generation stage, from my experience, having trained tens of thousands of people in Design Thinking, is the hardest stage to master. To get good at this does literally take the 10 000 hours of practice. When beginners run this stage, what you get is a list of matter-of-fact statements about the customer, lacking any real emotional insight. It leaves you thinking, 'So what?' To cap it all off, we have non–research professionals running the 'test' stage, leaving you with little real confidence as to whether the concepts are truly desirable to the customer, and whether they would even use and pay for the new solution. While some of this can be chalked up to teething problems, if people don't know any better then they will continue to make the same mistakes. Doing a few 'street intercepts' (where you walk up to a stranger on the street and ask them if you can interview them for five minutes about a common problem such as transportation), as they are often called in Design Thinking boot camps, doesn't prepare you for planning and running a full discovery or customer empathy phase on a high-profile innovation or customer experience project back at the office.

The other weakness with Design Thinking is that it over promises to deliver desirable, feasible and viable (DVF) solutions (see figure 3). Any successful innovation needs to be all three. People need to want it (desirable), and the organisation needs to be able to technically and organisationally make it (feasible) and make money from it (viable).

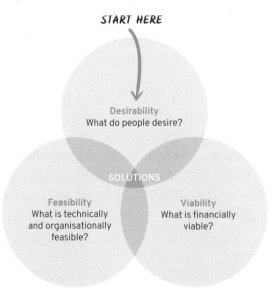

Figure 3: DVF innovation model

However, I've only ever seen the Design Thinking process take solutions as far as desirability, which is its strength. Design Thinking alone doesn't go into feasibility and viability. As you can see, in figure 4 a standard Design Thinking process, feasibility and viability are not included.

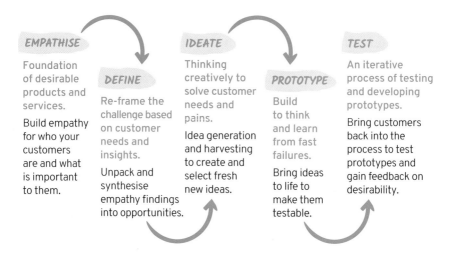

Figure 4: Design Thinking process diagram

To compensate for this, when I use Design Thinking I add some 'traditional' innovation tools and two other newer methodologies— Business Model Canvas and Lean Startup—to start developing feasible and viable concepts once I've already got a desirable solution.

BUSINESS MODEL GENERATION

Let's now take a look at the Business Model Canvas (see figure 5) developed by Alexander Osterwalder, Yves Pigneur and a large number of co-creators. While none of the nine elements of the Business Model Canvas are new, the innovation is in the reconfiguration of them into a one-page canvas. This new framework has led to the reemergence of business model thinking in innovation and design.

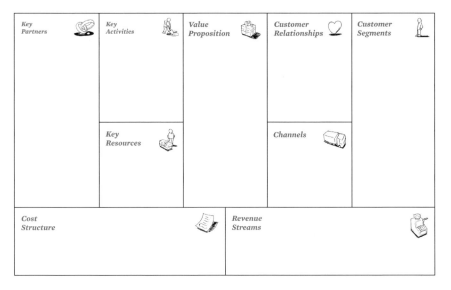

Figure 5: Business Model Canvas

Source: Alexander Osterwalder and Yves Pigneur, *Business Model Generation* (Hoboken, New Jersey: John Wiley & Sons, 2010)

What I really like about the Business Model Canvas is that it provides a tool and mindset for mapping out and experimenting with different business models for your solutions and enables you to prototype and then test different business models quickly and cheaply.

But this tool can also be misused, particularly when it is used to map out a business model for a solution without first knowing who the customer is and the problem they are solving. Until you've identified a problem that customers want to see solved, and you've tested that your solution solves this problem, then any efforts to develop a business model, even as quick as the canvas is, are wasted. Many examples and demonstrations of the Business Model Canvas start with the value proposition (the solution) and work back to the customer segment. It is not good innovation practice, to try and retrofit a customer problem to a preconceived solution. From experience, this 'solution looking for a problem' approach rarely works.

LEAN STARTUP

Lean Startup, which grew out of Lean Manufacturing, is a method for developing businesses and products. It aims to reduce product development time and rapidly discover if a proposed business model is feasible and viable. It provides a great method for narrowing down options based on evidence of what works and what doesn't — validating hypotheses by running experiments. Like the methodologies reviewed above, it has added considerably to the field of innovation and entrepreneurship.

What I love about Lean Startup is that it has the ability to help us develop feasible and viable solutions by flowing on from Design Thinking and integrating with the Business Model Canvas. My criticism of Lean Startup is that it starts with the solution (I've got an idea) and then searches for a problem to meet the solution and get what they call problem-solution fit, which, given the reverse engineering nature of this approach, should probably be called solution-problem fit! So the Lean Startup, which like the others has a fantastic suite of tools, encourages jumping to the solution. Budding innovators and entrepreneurs who learn this approach first then think this is how it is done and just keep pivoting when it turns out their solution has no problem to solve. Unfortunately, at some stage you have to exit the pivot stage and launch something.

Where I think Lean Startup can really add value to innovation is when it's used after you've achieved problem-solution fit by starting with customer needs through a Design Thinking approach.

AGILE DEVELOPMENT

Agile Development, which arose from technology and software development, is a program management methodology that uses short, time-boxed cycles called 'sprints' to focus on continuous improvement in the development of a product, experience or service, allowing faster execution and delivery to customers. Agile is now increasingly being adopted by other non-technology business functions.

My critique of Agile is not of it as a program management methodology. As an innovation adviser the problem I'm seeing is organisations and teams adopting Agile, but without having the front end of product development—discovery, insight, ideation, prototyping and testing—in place first. They are starting with an invalidated idea and jumping straight to Agile (maybe after getting signoff on a business case) to build and launch. In many cases these organisations just build the wrong products, experiences and services, but now faster! Due to our human nature of jumping to the solution and senior leaders' desire to get on with it and build and launch, this has resulted in the widespread adoption of Agile before the adoption and implementation of front-end methodologies like Design Thinking and Business Model Generation.

***

People need to develop skills with these methodologies beyond the two-day boot camp level. To increase the chances of successful innovation, people need to be taught and gain deeper experiences in the skills and tools, and how these methods work together, and in what sequence to apply them to innovation and design. Senior management need to develop better skills at leading the less predictable and more ambiguous and complex front end of innovation and learn what to measure and how to measure (develop new metrics) to help them to understand:

» how these methods are helping them create successful new products, experiences and services

» if they are on track.

My method for integrating Design Thinking, Business Model Canvas and Lean Startup is depicted in figure 6 (overleaf). Following Design Thinking and the prototyping and testing of solutions to see if they are desirable, we add the Business Model Canvas to map out the feasibility and viability elements of your solution. We then iterate between the Business Model Canvas and Lean Startup–style 'Build (Prototype), Measure (Test) and Learn' to run experiments to de-risk and validate the solution and business model.

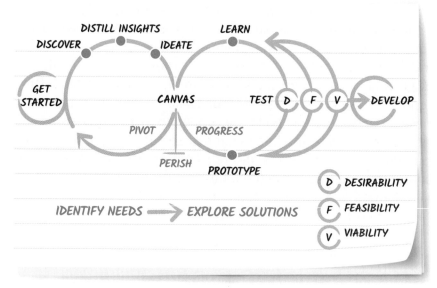

Figure 6: integrated design-led innovation

Read on for the guidance and robust framework you need to complement your enthusiasm and build on your skills, so you are no longer armed and dangerous, but armed and powerful.

Learnings

- 'Design' has changed in meaning; what used to primarily describe occupations held by creatives, it now describes any role that includes the design of a tangible or intangible artefact, for example, 'service designer', 'user experience designer'.

- There are no shortcuts in innovation. Jumping to the solution or, worse still, development, typically results in more defects, rework and costly failures.

- Getting the upfront stages of the innovation process right ensures you develop superior, unique and relevant products, services and experiences.

- A stitch in time saves nine — investing in the upfront stages of innovation actually saves you time and money in the long run by making the back end of the innovation journey more efficient and effective.

- Senior management should be educated as to the benefits of not jumping to the solution and getting the front end of innovation right in order to increase innovation success and speed to market.

- Innovation is a cross-functional team sport, and success in innovation requires a multidisciplinary team, from research to strategy to innovation and design to sales and marketing to finance and legal and so on.

- Design Thinking is a great methodology for developing desirable solutions. Coupled with Business Model Thinking and Lean Startup (and in that order), these three methods together are great for developing desirable, feasible and viable concepts.

- Don't make up your customer needs and insights. Too many organisations still believe they can brainstorm what the customer's needs are.

- Uncovering what really matters to your target customers requires deep qualitative research.

- If you start your innovation process off with Lean Startup or Agile before you've identified a customer problem that needs solving, and a solution that solves that problem, then you'll most often end up just building the wrong products faster.

Questions for innovators and leaders

- Do all your innovation and design projects currently start with researching and identifying who the customer is and what problems (needs) need solving?

- Do you know your capability strengths and gaps in the front end of innovation?

- Do you engage specialists for specialist tasks such as qualitative research?

- Are you currently investing enough time and resources to get the front end of innovation right?

- Do you validate concepts for DVF before they go into business case and development?

1

GET
STARTED

Before you start your project you'll need to assemble a crack multidisciplinary team and clearly define the opportunity area you want to innovate. You'll tighten up its focus and scope, getting alignment with your team, sponsor and key stakeholders. Finally, you'll have fun designing a space to play home for your team. In this stage you will learn how to set up for success.

So you've decided to go on an innovation journey. How do you set yourself and your team up for success on a journey that will be unpredictable, complex and ambiguous at times, and iterative, not linear, in nature? Before you dive into the real work of identifying customer needs you need to make sure you and your team are ready to get started.

You'll need to assemble a crack multidisciplinary team and clearly define the opportunity space you want to innovate. Then you'll tighten up the focus and scope of the opportunity space, getting alignment with your team, sponsors and key stakeholders. Finally, you'll have fun designing a space to play home base for your team as you do this work.

In this chapter I'll show you how to set yourself up for success. (Keep in mind this chapter isn't meant to be a replacement for good project management —you'll need that too— or the development of a proper innovation strategy.)

PREPARING YOUR TEAM

Innovation is a team sport. I liken it to team orienteering rather than a relay race. Not only is the orienteering trail more unpredictable than an athletics track, it also requires the team to work together side by side to navigate their way around the course, unlike handing over a baton to the next runner in a relay. Too often in organisations we work in our siloed departments, doing handovers from one team to the next. At each handover we risk losing the integrity of the original insights and ideas, as each team intentionally or unintentionally adds their own spin or flavour to the solution.

TEAM MAKEUP

Just like a sports team you're going to need an experienced cross-functional team with a variety and depth of skills to complete the wide range of tasks required to develop a new innovation. Having a 'true cross-functional team' is fifth in Cooper's top nine success factors of innovation, as discussed in the section, **My journey of discovery to innovation flow**.

You also want diversity to ensure expansive thinking, insights and ideas, as well as connection to different networks, both internally and externally. Having a multidisciplinary team will help with this, but you also want diversity of backgrounds, cultures, gender, age and mindset.

Ideally you'll have a core team of around six to ten people. The bigger your team gets the harder it's going to be to schedule meetings, especially if the project is in addition to your day job. According to Head of Innovation at Method, an eco-friendly cleaning product company, Joshua Handy, one of the biggest killers of innovation is 'having to schedule a meeting and create a PowerPoint presentation'. The components of this team will vary by industry, but will likely include a:

» project 'innovation' leader

» project manager (highly recommended)

» research specialist

» marketing specialist

» sales specialist

» development/technology specialist

» packaging specialist

» supply chain specialist

» finance specialist

» design specialist.

Often the project leader is also one of the functional specialists. Having a dedicated project manager means everyone can focus on their specialist roles and leave the project management to the project manager. These people will be engaged throughout the project journey, not just for their specific functional expertise.

You'll also need a project sponsor. Whether the innovation project is full time or in addition to your day job, you are going to need senior sponsorship to provide project legitimacy, ground cover, free up the necessary time and resources, make connections and remove barriers.

In addition to the core team you'll have a 'bench' of subject matter experts and suppliers that you'll need to draw on from time to time, for example legal, customer recruitment agencies, visualisers and facilitators. The facilitator will guide you through the key workshops and possibly even facilitate the entire journey. It is important the facilitator stays neutral about decisions, so as to encourage everyone's input. For this reason the project leader should not be the facilitator. This book is written as if directed to the innovation leader or facilitator, but is equally useful to anyone interested in designing and running a better innovation journey to create innovations your customers will love.

TEAM PERFORMANCE

Just like a sports team, you won't win at innovation if you haven't got a cohesive and high-performing team. Even if on paper it is the best list of experts anyone could muster, if they don't play well together, you won't succeed. We've all been on good and bad teams. Table 1.1 shows some of their characteristics.

Table 1.1: worst and best team characteristics

Worst	Best
Political	Imaginative
Personal agendas are pursued	Trusting
Directionless	Respectful
Error prone	Innovative
High conflict	Fun
No personal growth	Roles are clear
Self-centred	Supportive
Prone to blame	Good leadership
	Flexible

We can look at team development and performance through the 'forming to performing' model developed by Bruce Tuckman in 1965, as shown in figure 1.1.

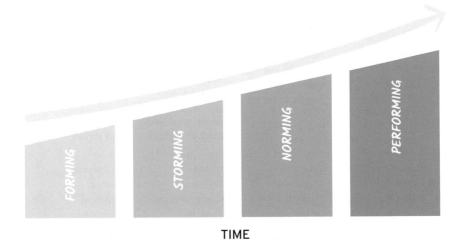

TIME

Figure 1.1: team development—stages
Source: Adapted from concepts by Bruce Tuckman

All newly formed teams go through forming, storming, norming and performing stages. All stages, according to Tuckman, are 'necessary and inevitable', so the key is to go through the first two stages before the project properly starts. This is a key objective of the 'Get Started' stage. Figure 1.2 (overleaf) goes into what each stage looks and feels like in more detail by looking at it from three different lenses:

1. act
2. think
3. feel.

FORMING	STORMING	NORMING	PERFORMING
ACT Floundering / Polite / Guarded	Aggressive / Resistant / Opting out / Cliques	Cohesion / Establishing systems / Confronting issues	Supportive / Flexible / Open / Trusting
THINK Why are we here? / What are we doing? / Who can I trust? / What is the purpose?	Who is in charge? / What are the issues? / Are we doing the right thing? / How will I get it done?	What are the tasks, deliverables and standards? / How will we manage work and report on status?	How can we be more innovative and high performing? / How can we better support each other?
FEEL Uncomfortable / Uncertain / Confused	Confronting / Angry / Frustrated / On the outer	Cohesive / Positive / Making progress / Respected	Empowered / Trusted / Confident / Recognition

Figure 1.2: team development—how they act, think and feel by stage

Source: Adapted from concepts by Bruce Tuckman

By understanding these stages, the essentials for good teamwork and what a successful team looks like, we can look to accelerate team development. Some key essentials for a high-functioning team, identified from both Tuckman's work and my own experience, are:

» a clear goal

» a sense of drive/passion

» agreement on priorities

» deadlines/deliverables

» ownership of decisions and/or a bias towards action

» communication

» trust

» helpfulness between team members

» commitment/dedication

» information sharing

» a team to play against.

A successful team:

» likes working together

» communicates the bad news

» argues/challenges each other

» trusts each other

» knows what each other are doing

» actively shares information

» communicates all the time

» respects the contribution of others

» wants to win.

We can accelerate team development through:

» pre-project preparation

» a project kick-off workshop

» team building events

» clarifying individual roles

» managing conflict constructively.

Once you've selected your team you can accelerate team development at your project kick-off workshop and by running a fun team-building event either at the beginning or end of the workshop.

TIPS

Taking new methodologies into new teams, locations or organisations can be met with some resistance. Human beings don't always initially respond well to change. Business Design and Integrative Thinking expert Roger Martin has some good tips for applying customer-centric innovation in new or hostile territories:

» Reframe extreme views as a creative challenge and apply the method to solve for them.

» Empathise with your colleagues on extremes (those who are invested in traditional analytical business thinking and new Design Thinking).

» Learn to speak the languages of both extremes.

» Step back from perfection (and don't be a zealot).

» Turn the future into the past by validating through experiments.

DEFINING THE CHALLENGE AND PLANNING THE PROJECT

Now it's time to discuss what you'll be diving into—your innovation challenge!

Before starting a project with a client or internal team I ask them to complete a project brief on a provided template. Not only does this give me a better chance of successfully meeting their needs, it is also a good test of their commitment to the project. After all, if they can't make the time to complete the brief then it probably isn't worth pursuing. Sometimes I help them by interviewing them about the project, using the template as a discussion guide. I write it up and send it back to them for review and sign-off. Other times I run a project kick-off meeting with the newly formed team to complete each of the elements; this can only happen if I've already had at least an initial briefing from the project sponsor. In this case, after the workshop I would take the sponsor through the write-up for review and sign-off. The elements I like to cover in the project brief, which you can tailor and add to, are:

1. *What success looks like.* What's our end goal, why are we doing this, what are the key objectives and deliverables?

2. *Challenge statement.* What's our single-minded, positive and exciting project definition?

3. *Target customer.* Who are we solving for?

4. *Scope.* What's in scope and out of scope?

5. *Existing ideas and hypotheses.* What existing ideas, development work or hypotheses should we explore?

6. *Existing research and background materials.* What background materials are relevant to immerse the team in? What existing research has been done on the opportunity space you are exploring?

7. *Constraints.* Is there anything we definitely can't change?

8. *Barriers.* Are there obstacles we need to be aware of and manage?

9. *Stakeholders.* Who are our key stakeholders?

10. *Timing and budget.* When does this need to go live by? What budget is set aside and signed off?

A critical element in the project brief is a clearly defined and engaging challenge. We can't be all things to all people, and every organisation and project has limited time and resources. It may sound counterintuitive, but creativity and innovation actually love focus. Clearly articulating an opportunity first actually better allows people to unleash their creativity within that space. 'Focus and simplicity' were also one of Steve Jobs's mantras, and who are we to argue with the great man? So we need to decide early where we are going to focus those resources and where we are not.

TIP

The challenge statement should come from your briefing by the sponsor—but let your team modify it if they have good cause. It also helps with team buy-in, and can lead to a better articulation.

PROJECT KICK-OFF WORKSHOP

In the project kick-off, a good starting agenda that you can modify to your challenge is the following:

1. Welcome
2. Introductions
3. Energiser and/or team building exercise
4. The agenda
5. Project introduction
6. Team organisation and roles
7. Project brief elements (from the previous section)
8. Project planning
9. Risk analysis
10. Future meetings and actions.

THE INNOVATION OPPORTUNITY

Your team should be starting with a prioritised innovation opportunity that has been briefed to you by your sponsor. Or if you're an intrapreneur or entrepreneur it may be an opportunity area you've uncovered or have a passion for. What I mean by 'innovation opportunity' is a large, well-defined space for growth, within the organisation's overall growth and innovation strategy, that needs to be explored and developed further through the innovation process to be realised. An innovation opportunity:

» is a level or two higher than an idea

» is a space for innovation that should lead to several customer-centric sub-opportunities and ideas

» should inspire ideas, but not have an idea baked into it

» could be a trend, technology, market insight, customer group, customer occasion or a combination of these

» is framed with the end customer in mind.

Here are some example innovation opportunities:

» *Financial services organisation.* How might we better meet the financial needs of the growing small business market?

» *Airline.* How might we improve the long-haul travel experience?

» *Fitness organisation.* How might we better meet the fitness needs of the youth market?

» *Food manufacturer.* How might we better serve healthy, busy families?

» *Smart phone company.* How might we better meet the needs of people with active lifestyles?

» *Cycling company.* How might we get more women riding?

» *Government organisation.* How might we encourage more people to vote?

» *HR team.* How might we improve the onboarding experience?

As I've mentioned, this chapter isn't a replacement for proper innovation strategy development or portfolio management. They're topics worthy of a book themselves. Therefore, in this chapter I won't be addressing how to uncover strategic high-level opportunities for growth like the examples above. What I'll be focusing on in this section is how to frame up these already-identified opportunities to get your innovation journey off to a good start. If you don't have an innovation strategy and opportunity area to focus on, then it's worth taking a step back and deciding where you want to play first and why. This might involve engaging your strategy and research teams to do an environmental scan and then analyse and identify some sizeable opportunities that will unlock growth and fit with your organisation's overall strategy.

TIP

I recommend working on one innovation opportunity at a time, with up to four teams working in parallel on it. Having four teams work on a challenge simultaneously gives you different ways into the opportunity space and ways of solving it. You can run this by giving each team a different focus, for example a different customer segment or occasion.

MAKE IT DEFINED AND ENGAGING

So you have your prioritised innovation opportunity. Now we need to ensure it's clearly defined and engaging.

We start by clarifying the challenge and then we rephrase it to ensure it is customer-centric, inspiring and engaging.

Some tools we use to help us clarify the challenge in the kick-off workshop are:

1. Focus: zoom in and zoom out

2. Scope

and a tool we use for clearly articulating the challenge is:

3. Rephrase the challenge.

1. FOCUS: ZOOM IN AND ZOOM OUT

 TIME
15–25 minutes

 PEOPLE
Core team of 6–10

 MATERIALS
A whiteboard/flip chart paper, markers and sticky notes

1. Draw a funnel on flip chart paper or a whiteboard.

2. Write your current challenge statement (probably from your sponsor) on a sticky note and place it in the middle of your funnel.

3. Now generate new statements by zooming in—capturing each iteration on sticky notes and plotting on the flip chart paper or whiteboard.

In order to zoom in try asking:

- How are we going to do this?
- What are the parts of this?

4. Now generate new statements by zooming out—capturing each iteration on sticky notes and plotting on the flip chart paper or whiteboard.

In order to zoom out try asking:

- Why are we doing this?
- What is this a part of?

5. Once you have settled on the right level, highlight it on your flip chart paper or whiteboard.

The higher up the funnel the more dollars, time and resources you'll need. The lower down the funnel the closer it gets to being a solution and not an opportunity.

For example, let's imagine we are working for an airline and the innovation opportunity area is 'improving the long-haul flying experience', as shown in figure 1.3.

Figure 1.3: zooming in and out on long-haul flights

We zoom in by asking how we might do this and what are the parts of this. This leads to us narrowing our focus and we might come up with 'improving the long-haul in-flight experience' or go even narrower, like 'improving the seats'. The first one sounds acceptable, assuming we know from research that there is room to improve the in-flight experience. Improving seats is starting to sound like a solution. But we haven't actually premeditated how to improve the seats. Whereas, if we said 'improve the seats by increasing the width by 30 millimetres' then this would be a solution and we are being too specific.

We then zoom out, asking 'why are we doing this?' and 'what is this a part of?'. We might come up with 'to gain competitor advantage' and, even broader, 'to increase customer loyalty'. Now these two are getting too broad and abstract. While they might be the beginnings of good project objectives, they're not specific enough for a project.

Let's say we then go back to our sponsor and say that we feel 'improving the long-haul flying experience' would be a huge undertaking as one project, and recommend breaking it down into multiple projects with a steering group overseeing all the projects. We suggest the project could be broken down into:

» planning and booking the trip

» travel to the airport and checking in and pre-departure

» boarding the flight and flying

» arrival and getting to your first destination.

Hopefully from this example you can see that there is a sliding scale that you are playing with, from being too broad and abstract at the top to too specific, narrow and almost a solution at the bottom. You want your challenge to be in the sweet spot, or what I like to call the 'Goldilocks zone'. Also, depending on resourcing you may need to move lower down the funnel.

2. SCOPE

	TIME		PEOPLE		MATERIALS
	15–25 minutes		Core team of 6–10		A whiteboard/flip chart paper, markers and sticky notes

Now that you have the right level of focus it is important to clarify further where to focus—what's in scope and out of scope for the project? 'Scoping' helps you clarify this.

1. Draw or create a vertical line on the wall, table or floor. Label the left side of the line as 'in scope' and right side as 'out of scope'.

2. Write as many questions about the focus of the project as you and your team can in five minutes. You can be quite prescriptive to ensure you cover all avenues by using a framework such as 5W: Who for? When/Where? Why? What? For example, 'Are families in scope?' 'Is breakfast in scope?' And reviewing the whole supply chain and/or business model, for example 'Is retail in or out of scope?' 'Is frozen food in scope?' Write one question per piece of paper or sticky note.

3. Each team member takes it in turn to ask the project owner whether their question is in or out of scope.

4. The project owner answers by placing the question in or out. (No question can be placed on the line. It is either in or out.) It will look something like figure 1.4.

5. Write it up as part of your project challenge and scoping.

Figure 1.4: scoping

Back to our airline example, we unpack through this process that the audience (who) is families who can afford to travel long haul, but aren't (why) and the occasion/journey stage (when and where) is the in-flight experience. At this stage all potential in-flight solutions are in scope (what).

3. REPHRASE THE CHALLENGE

TIME 15–25 minutes	**PEOPLE** Core team of 6–10	**MATERIALS** A whiteboard/flip chart paper, markers and sticky notes

Once we feel we are at the right level of focus and we know what is in and out of scope, we then turn to phrasing the challenge in the right way to inspire and engage people's natural creativity.

1. Start by writing the challenge in the 'How might we … ' (HMW) format. Our brains are more likely to solve problems if we phrase them as questions. HMW also encourages us to believe that the challenge can be solved.

2. Then make sure it is positive. A negative sentence can take a lot more brain power to deal with. Positive statements are much more motivating.

3. Next, write the challenge in a customer-centric way. We want our challenges to be focused on uncovering and solving real customer needs.

4. Check that the challenge statement:
    - truly excites you
    - has no solutions baked in
    - has no jargon.

5. Write up your final challenge statement.

For example, there is an old story of a Toyota executive who asked employees to come up with 'ways to increase their productivity', but recieved only blank stares in response.

However, when they instead asked 'How might we make your jobs easer?' they were flooded with suggestions.

> **TIP**
>
> Our brains love questions. The more engrossing the question is, the harder our brains will work to answer it. This problem solving begins immediately and continues, whether we are conscious of it or not (incubating).

Returning to the airline example, our rephrased airline innovation challenge then becomes something like:

How might we improve the in-flight experience on long-haul travel for families with young children and a low propensity to travel, so they can enjoy the benefits of travel?

WRITE UP FINAL PROJECT CHALLENGE AND BRIEF

We use the project brief template to capture all key information about the challenge, forcing important questions to be asked upfront and to align the team. Key sponsors and stakeholders should then sign this off before progressing. The briefing template is continually referenced, to see how the project is tracking versus the original objectives.

DESIGNING A PHYSICAL SPACE

Innovation is a much more visual and 'solve by doing' approach than most business as usual projects. You're standing, creating, writing with markers on sticky notes and working in groups. Some might call it messy due to the number of sticky notes, butcher paper, whiteboards, prototypes and so on in use and on display. Often, in business as usual projects, we try and think of the solution before we build. Our workspaces tend to be a desk with a computer in an open plan office, and meeting rooms where we talk, not do. Whereas in innovation we borrow from 'designers'—solving by doing and making. You need a space that not only enables this, but also encourages these behaviours. You also need at least three times as much space per person as you'd normally allow for in a meeting room. Innovation can be as much about the space and artefacts you use as the methods and tools. As Joshua Handy, head of Innovation at Method cleaning products, said,

> ... we try to think of design as a culture rather than a strategy. ... we have a culture that is all about design so part of that is about collaboration, communication, and transparency. When we walk around the office, everyone's thinking is on the walls.

So what does this actually look like?

WALL SPACE

You'll need plenty of wall space and/or whiteboards for completing your innovation activities. I actually find having both is great, and you can use the whiteboards as movable and usable walls between each team zone. I'll have more on breaking your project team up into sub-teams in stage 4: Ideate, but for now it is worth considering you'll want space for up to four sub-teams during key workshops. You'll find that just about every stage of the front end of innovation journey uses templates and canvases that are populated with insights and ideas on sticky notes. It is far easier doing this and visualising it on a wall. It also gets you on your feet, which means you have more energy. There'll be other times for sitting down. Think of it like a TV detective's workspace as they're trying to solve a crime. The space should:

» encourage action and solving by doing

» signal failure is okay

» have a designated space for making simple, quick and low-cost mock-ups (prototypes) of products

» have acoustic, not visual, separation between team zones. So it is more 'car garage' than 'car showroom'.

PERMANENCY

You'll also need your thinking and artefacts to stay up. You are going to be evolving and iterating these. Having to take them down at the end of every day, store them and then find a new room the next day and repeat it over and over again will just result in lost ideas and wasted time and energy. Time that should be going into understanding your customers and innovating! Having your customers' insights and ideas up permanently on a wall (until project completion) also makes it easier for stakeholder walk-throughs and showcases. So get permission for a dedicated space.

PLENARY SPACE

You'll also need a central space for the team to get together and instruct tasks to others in workshops and so on. This is where seating is suitable. You can go with just chairs, add tables, or make it more relaxed, with couches and beanbags. Just remember, design it for how you want to use the space.

It is also great to put everything on wheels. When Stanford's d.school redesigned their space they took inspiration from the stage in performing arts. Everything was made movable — walls, whiteboards, even the couches were on wheels. It makes you want to dive straight in and do stuff. No obstacle is a barrier.

Hopefully you've found this section on getting started useful. But if you're like me you're probably itching to get into it. Next, in stage 2, it'll be time to dive in and immerse yourselves into the world of the customer.

Learnings

- Minimise innovation failure and mistakes through poor handovers between teams and silos by running cross-functional teams that work side by side. Involve the designers, developers and other BEI (back end of innovation) resources early in the journey.

- Innovation loves focus. Have a clear challenge you are trying to solve. This is best served through having an innovation strategy, which consists of clear innovation opportunity areas.

- Make sure your challenge statement is customer-centric. Remember that, while you might be starting with a business challenge, unless you are improving the customer's life in some way it is unlikely to be successful.

- Get your team performing and collaborating as early as possible in the project through preparation, team building exercises, clear roles and responsibilities and managing conflict constructively.

- Find and designate a willing senior leader to be the project's champion. This needs to be someone who can provide project legitimacy, ground cover, free up the necessary time and resources, make connections and remove barriers.

Questions for innovators and leaders

- Does your organisation and/or division have an innovation strategy that outlines the key opportunities for growth? What are they and how are you working towards fulfilling them?

- How do you currently set your innovation teams up for success? Do you put experienced project leaders and managers on the more difficult and disruptive innovation projects and groom less experienced team members on core and incremental projects? While also keeping a mix of exuberant youth and experience across all projects?

- Do you run your innovation projects with cross-functional teams, or siloed teams with handovers?

- Do you apply effort and focus to team dynamics and performance, or are teams just expected to get on with it? What can you learn from successful high-performing teams such as sports teams?

- Is there space in your organisation for people to conduct the messy, tactile and visual front end of innovation?

2

DISCOVER

In stage one, you and your team defined the opportunity area you want to focus on and then crafted this into a customer-centric challenge statement. In stage two you'll immerse yourselves in the world of the customer to explore this opportunity area from a customer lens to identify opportunities to improve people's lives.

Here's my recipe for disaster:

» Lock yourself in a garage, lab or some other secluded and isolated space and work solo, or as an insular team, for days, weeks, months or even years on some new bright idea!

» Focus on making sure it works technically!

» Make sure you don't share your idea with anyone in case they copy it and launch it before you.

» Definitely do not test it with potential customers.

» Brief the media to launch it to the world for you.

» Tell them to talk about how innovative it is, how it will advance humankind, how it's the biggest breakthrough since sliced bread, but don't, no matter how persistent they are with their questions, tell them what it actually is. That's your best chance of surprising the market.

Your innovation might be new and it will be sure to work, but will anyone want it? The answer is most likely no. Why, you ask? Because more startups and innovations fail from a lack of customers (desirability) than from a failure of the product or technology itself.

To increase your chances of success you need to start with the problem, not the solution, by uncovering true customer needs and insights. And not the sort made up in the office. Even if you use an insight capture tool such as personas, customer profiles or empathy maps you are still just guessing unless you talk to customers first. You have to actually go out and discover insights through customer research and empathy. As Steve Blank, Silicon Valley entrepreneur and founder of the customer development method that launched the Lean Startup movement says, 'real-life insights don't live in your office; they exist out in the world of your customers and potential customers'. You have to get out of the building (GOOB). You begin your innovation journey proper by building empathy for:

» who your customers are

» what is important to them

» what pains them and what delights them.

Empathy is the ability to understand and share the feelings of another. Empathy:

» *gives you understanding.* How can you innovate for someone you don't have empathy for?

» *leads to the development of real-world insights.* How many times have you been in a meeting or workshop where, as a team, you create (make up) the customer insights and needs for the product, service or brand activity you are developing? We want real-world insights, not the sort made up in the ivory tower

» *deeply motivates teams.* Getting your teams out of the ivory tower into the real world to meet with your customers and becoming deeply immersed into their lives generates higher motivation in teams

» *gives meaning.* Empathising with your customers enables you to identify problems worthy of solving! It gives meaning to your job and a reason to come to work

» *increases the chance of success.* Too many organisations waste their time inventing products and services for non-existent needs.

There are also some great behaviours to adopt during your research. The best researchers exhibit the following behaviours:

» *Curiosity.* They have a sense of wonder and excitement about everything. A lust for discovery and a questioning mind.

» *Empathy.* They see the world through the eyes of other people.

» *Objectivity.* They put aside what they know. They do not impose their worldview on the facts or analysis.

» *Eyes and ears.* They soak up all information available. They listen and look and explore. Everything is a source of insight.

» *Rapport.* They build a strong rapport with their customers.

» *Respect.* They respect the people they are observing and interviewing.

In this chapter I'll share a structured approach, with the tools, skills and behaviours required for empathy and customer immersion, equipping you to constantly anticipate and meet customer needs.

In the Discover stage I'll help you:

» clarify what you know and don't know about your customers

» validate and invalidate hypotheses about your customers

» discover fresh findings about your customers.

All this will be fed into the next stage.

The steps to building empathy for who your customers are and what is important to them are:

1. conducting a knowledge review

2. doing fresh empathy research

3. distilling key observations and findings.

1. CONDUCTING A KNOWLEDGE REVIEW

The knowledge review has three purposes. It:

1. identifies what we know

2. identifies what we don't know

3. allows us to formulate any hypotheses that we'd like to test.

Let's start with what you know. It is important that you don't commission fresh research every time you start a new project; first see what you already know or have on the opportunity space and customer. You can do this by:

» reviewing all the existing research your organisation has on the opportunity and customer

» interviewing people within the organisation who know a lot about this space to gleam knowledge from them; you'll find these 'wise heads' across the organisation, both horizontally and vertically, as well as key subject matter experts

» go online and see what you can find that already exists on your opportunity space.

A useful tool I use to frame what has already been uncovered on the opportunity is the 5W tool. I use it to capture what we know and where there are gaps—questions that still need to be explored in new research. The 5W knowledge review asks:

» Who?

 − Who is the target market for this opportunity?

 − What do we know about them and their lifestyle?

» When?

 − What are the occasions (e.g. breakfast, date night, barbecue) within this opportunity?

 − When are they consuming?

» Where?

 − Where are they consuming?

» Why?

- What are their needs?

- Why do they purchase and consume?

» What?

- What do they currently consume?

- What are their likes and frustrations with the current offering?

Another great tool and exercise for reviewing and capturing existing knowledge and research is the Re-sight Tool (shown in figure 2.1), where you:

1. Collate existing research, desk research and interview notes from internal knowledge (wise head) interviews through these four lenses, which help you consider the full picture:

   i. the world

   ii. the market

   iii. your organisation

   iv. the end customer.

2. Divide the sources among your team to review using the Resight Tool (see figure 2.1) to capture:

   i. existing but important knowledge

   ii. new knowledge

   iii. knowledge gaps

   iv. early hunches and ideas.

3. Create a fieldwork brief (research plan and customer interview guide) to fill the knowledge gaps, explore the hypotheses and gain greater empathy with your end customers (from the right-hand side boxes). The outputs from the left-hand side boxes are kept for later and brought back in at stage 3: Distill insights.

CONFIRMS

Confirms what we know, but it is important to remind ourselves of it.

KNOWLEDGE GAPS

Things we don't know and still need to understand.

DISCOVERIES

New facts or insights.

HYPOTHESES AND IDEAS

Would like to explore.

Figure 2.1: Re-sight Tool

2. DOING FRESH EMPATHY RESEARCH

As former colleague and insights guru Steven Melford says, 'Ask the same questions of the same people in the same ways and you'll get the same old findings'.

This stage is about filling your knowledge gaps around the opportunity space by focusing on who your customer is in real life and what is important to them. It seeks to complement the existing research and knowledge you gathered in the previous step.

When you are creating new products, services and experiences, or even evolving existing ones, you are looking for fresh insights—the untapped, latent needs that no-one else has discovered yet. To discover fresh insights is difficult and requires applying a different angle to your research. It actually requires you to be quite creative in your approach.

This is where exploring multiple sources of research can be really beneficial. Just like detectives will pursue multiple lines of enquiry to solve a crime, we need to pursue multiple lines of customer enquiry to solve an innovation challenge. While traditional focus groups are an efficient and effective way of doing research and a great start point, they are only one source. Exploring multiple sources usually results in new and more compelling insights.

Therefore, to unlock unique untapped insights we need to apply different types of qualitative research methods, including:

» ethnographic and observational research

» in-depth interviews

» extreme customers

» techniques such as deprivation and disruption.

EXTREME CUSTOMERS

A great way to get the fresh insights that you are looking for in design and innovation projects is to talk to extreme customers. By observing and talking to extreme customers you find the experience is heightened for them, so you uncover insights that you wouldn't get by talking to just mainstream customers—yet the insights are still applicable to the masses. Extreme customers are not your mainstream customer base. For a breakfast food company 'extreme customers' might be the health junkie or the breakfast skipper. For a gaming company they might be the 19-year-old hacker who lives in their parents' basement at one extreme and the grandfather who doesn't even own a smartphone at the other. One good way to identify extreme customers is through the bell curve. Figure 2.2 shows how extreme customers are distributed.

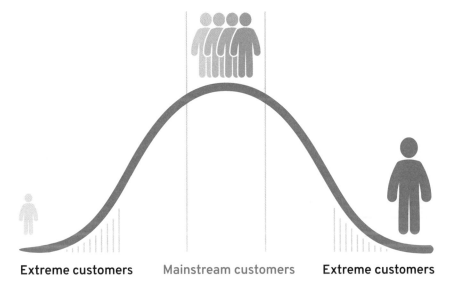

Extreme customers   Mainstream customers   **Extreme customers**

Figure 2.2: distribution of extreme customers

Take Zyliss for example, the maker of amazingly designed kitchen tools and gadgets. One of the co-facilitators I run Design Thinking and Innovation training workshops with tells the story of how Zyliss redesigned the pizza cutter. They got groups of grandparents and grandchildren together to do some cooking (these were their 'extreme customers'). They observed that the grandparents and grandchildren really struggled to cut through the base of the pizza with a traditional pizza cutter. Most of them wanted to put more weight down onto the pizza cutter with their other hand, but couldn't because of the design; they'd cut their hand. Based on these observations Zyliss were able to redesign the pizza cutter to allow the customer to safely put more force onto the blade with either one or both hands. Now, whether you're a child or a fully-grown adult, you'd probably like an easier way to cut pizza. Yet if Zyliss had only watched normal adults they might not have as easily picked up on the difficulty people have cutting pizza. This is a great example of how insights that are helpful for everyone can be uncovered by extreme customers. So when planning the research phase of your project, have a think about who the extreme customers are. And don't just interview them; observe them, like Zyliss did.

DEPRIVATION AND DISRUPTION

When you are innovating for a mature category, such as cereal or beer, it can be hard for customers to articulate any substantial unmet needs, frustrations or desires. This is where deprivation and disruption techniques can help.

Deprivation involves depriving the customer of a regular activity, product or brand and getting them to keep a diary of how it made them act, think and feel. Similar to the thinking behind researching extreme customers, this technique helps heighten the needs and pain points for the customer.

Disruption works well when you are innovating a physical or virtual space, or the product you're working on is central to a physical or virtual space. For example, if you were looking for insights to redesign a workplace you could get employees to go and work in a different space for a week and keep a diary of all the things they missed (and didn't miss) from their normal workspace, and what they liked and didn't like about the new workspace. Once again it creates a heightened experience, so the needs and pains more easily bubble to the surface.

MULTIPLE SOURCES FRAMEWORK

A tool I find to be really good for mapping out and planning these different types of research is the Multiple Sources Framework (see figure 2.3). The tool provides you and your team with a framework for both brainstorming and planning all the different types of qualitative research you could conduct for your project. It puts those sources of research under the lens of:

» being the customer

» being with the customer

» learning about the customer.

	BE THE CUSTOMER	BE WITH THE CUSTOMER	LEARN ABOUT THE CUSTOMER
MAINSTREAM	Experience the situation the customer experiences	Observe and talk to target customers	Talk to the people around them
EXTREME	Put yourself in the situations of extreme customers	Observe and talk to extreme customers	Talk to experts

Figure 2.3: Multiple Sources Framework

BE THE CUSTOMER

I love this technique. As I mentioned before, how can you innovate for someone you don't have empathy for? This technique is all about spending time being the customer—living in their shoes. Go and experience the situation the customer experiences. Spend 'a day in their life'. Go where they go (gym, bar, supermarket), watch the programs and films they do, read the websites, social media sites and magazines they do, use the products they use.

On one project we were redesigning the customer experience for Les Mills BodyPump class—the world's most popular barbell workout. Les Mills is the world leader for group fitness.

Now, to help us really build empathy for the customer and understand the pain points and delight points of a BodyPump experience, we attended a couple of classes each—going through the whole journey, from registering for the class through to waking the next day with sore muscles that we hadn't used for a long time.

During our experience we observed that a key sticking point in the whole BodyPump class experience was the mad scramble for equipment at the beginning of the class, then being surrounded by a mass of gear during the class, only to find out that you didn't have the right piece of equipment for the exercise being demonstrated by the instructor.

Our solution was the redesign of the weights system, creating an all-in-one exercise product. This decreased the complexity in setting up, and decreased the space required around each participant during the class. The new weight system also increased the flexibility and speed of changing equipment to match each exercise. We worked with the Les Mills team up until early prototyping and testing, following which the final design was completed by 4ormfunction, a product design company, and is now in use around the globe at thousands of fitness clubs and gyms.

On another project creating new breakfast products, experiences and services for families, we had team members who were single do the weekly shop for a friend's family, and vice versa, and have breakfast with each other in their homes. Spending time in your customer's shoes is a great way of building empathy for them and uncovering problems that you feel excited by and motivated to solve.

BE WITH THE CUSTOMER

Spending time with the customer is all about observing and interviewing them.

The teams I've been part of and worked with have completed an incredible volume and diversity of customer observations and interviews in our time. These types of activities are often called 'customer immersions' or 'customer connections'. Many of the large multinational FMCG companies like P&G, Unilever and Diageo have actually been doing this type of research for a long time, long before Design Thinking and Empathy Research became popular. I first got exposed to this type of research when I was working as a brand manager for Unilever's Wall's ice cream in London back in 2000. On one such consumer connection my team were booked in to meet some teenagers that fit our target audience after school (accompanied by their parents). We joined in on their after-school activities, were shown around their homes, talked through what they had for an after-school snack, went through their cupboards, fridge and freezer, and then went to the local corner shop to buy a treat. The insight we got from this exercise was that mobile phone cards (how pay-as-you-go mobile phones were topped up in the early 2000s) were the biggest threat to the teenage ice cream market. Kids were using their pocket money to top up their mobile phones rather than buy treats such as ice cream. We had to start thinking about different ways to engage with this audience and make our products more relevant in response to a disruptive threat.

There are literally thousands of exercises you can do in this space. I've gone supermarket shopping with customers, met them back at their house, watched them cook dinner and then had dinner with them. I've sent teams out to have breakfast with their customers, I've gone out for a day in the delivery van for a boutique coffee roaster and talked to their customers. The possibilities are just endless.

One time my colleague and I were researching primary school children to come up with new snack products for them. By sitting and watching the kids have morning tea and play (observation), we learned things that we wouldn't have in focus groups. For example, at recess they only get 15 minutes and they must sit down to eat their food in the first five minutes. But most primary-school-aged children are too small to finish a whole snack such as an apple in five minutes. If they are still sitting there finishing it after five minutes, then they are missing out on serious playtime with their friends and can even be teased for this. We also observed that if the snacks could be eaten one-handed then the kids could keep eating and still play on the jungle gyms or monkey bars, so they were still happy. This observation sparked a new insight and a whole lot of new and innovative ideas around one-handed kids' snacks at the ideation session.

LEARN ABOUT THE CUSTOMER

The third method is about interviewing and talking to people around the customer—people who know them best or will give you unique insights about them. They could be experts such as teachers, nutritionists, doctors and so on, but can also just be people who are close to them or observe them every day, such as family members or the school bus driver.

When working for a brand and innovation consultancy in London, one of our teams was tasked with re-launching Brylcreem—the British brand of hairstyling products for men first launched in 1928. As part of the discovery phase our team talked to the girlfriends and partners of the target audience, as they were more likely to tell us more about the grooming habits of the young guys we were targeting than they would tell us themselves! On the same project we also went to the hairdressers with the young guys and interviewed their hairstylists, while they were getting their haircut. The funniest thing was when a bald guy turned up for a research interview. I'm not sure how he got through the recruitment screener!

TIPS

» Conduct the research while it's still fresh with the customers, so they are almost still experiencing it and not struggling to remember it.

» Make use of stimulus such as hypotheses and ideas, as they give the customer something real to respond to. But don't test the hypotheses and ideas until towards the end of the interview, so as not to 'lead the witness'.

» Don't focus your customer segments too narrowly in the beginning. Cast a wide net with customers, but go deep. Run in-depth interviews with at least four to five customers per potential segment. This will help ensure you get good breadth and depth of lifestyles, needs and pain points. After four to five interviews in each segment you should start hearing recurring themes. Remember, though, at this stage you are looking for inspiration for innovation, not market validation.

» When you are out there in the field where the customer is situated (e.g. customers' homes, the supermarket), what you are looking for are the customer workarounds, obstacles to progress, undesired outcomes, risks, desires, tensions, contradictions, anomalies and simply just things that just stand out. However, don't lead the witness. I cover more on ways to run great observational and interview work later in this chapter.

MULTIPLE SOURCES FRAMEWORK EXERCISE

TIME
30–60 minutes

PEOPLE
Core team of 6–10

MATERIALS
A whiteboard/flip chart paper, markers and sticky notes

Here's how you brainstorm and plan your research activities using the Multiple Sources Framework.

1. Create a grid with headings (as per figure 2.3) on paper or a whiteboard.

2. Brainstorm empathy research activities for each quadrant under 'be them', 'be with them' and 'learn about them'.

3. Allocate activities to pairs within the group to go out into 'field' to conduct the research, which I'll explain how to do next.

CUSTOMER IMMERSION

The next steps for you and your team are to go and put your new empathy skills to use and uncover new insights by being, observing and interviewing customers, extreme customers and 'experts'. In preparation you've:

» identified what gaps and what questions you want answered from your Re-sight Tool and shaped these into a discussion guide (the list of topics you'd like to explore with the customer during your research interview, something your research team member can lead)

» completed the Multiple Sources Framework

» agreed which pairs are doing what and going where

» scheduled a time or date to check back in to see how each pair is going.

But before you charge off with your newfound empathy skills and energy, I have a few more tips for you in your fieldwork observation and interviews:

1. Interview in pairs.

2. Observe first.

3. Your introduction is important—it puts the participants at ease.

4. You are in control. Reinforce the positive, control the direction.

5. Employ a logical structure. Start broad, then probe deeper.

6. Ask open questions. Some questions are best not asked directly; open questions will prevent dead ends.

7. Seek stories.

8. Probe, probe, probe.

9. Give a helping hand. Use a stimulus or prompt if necessary.

10. Take notes during and after the fieldwork, but don't get distracted.

11. Be an objective sponge; leave your own beliefs at the door.

1. INTERVIEW IN PAIRS

Doing observation work and interviews in pairs is just such a great way to do it. You'll each pick up different observations and one of you can be the interviewer and the other can take notes. You'll also find you bounce off each other in the synthesis stage. It's safer for your own personal security and it's more fun. If you can't do it in pairs then going solo still works; you might want to consider recording the interview, and of course if at any time you feel unsafe before or during the research activity you should leave.

2. OBSERVE FIRST

When you can, observe your end customers in situ first. This will give you insights you won't get from interviewing them (like the primary school and Zyliss examples), provoke new hypotheses and questions that you can ask later, and it will give context to your current questions, as well as for your overall innovation project. This could include undisrupted observation (where you have no or little impact on the experience), as well as activities such as going shopping with them, having breakfast with them, going to the gym with them, followed up by a chat (interview).

3. YOUR INTRODUCTION IS IMPORTANT

Your introduction is important—it puts the customer at ease. You need to be comfortable and confident to achieve this. Practise and relax. Most often customers will never have been interviewed before and can find it intimidating. Outlining what they are here for and what's going to happen in a confident manner will alleviate this.

Try including the following points:

» Thanks for agreeing to chat.

» What's going to happen in the interview is ...

» What we're going to talk about is ...

» Everything is confidential.

» The interview will take about 60 minutes today.

» There is no right or wrong answer—everyone's opinion is valid.

» I need to keep us on time, so sometimes I might bring us back to a topic ...

» I'm taking notes as we go—but I am listening to everything you say.

4. YOU ARE IN CONTROL

You are in control—reinforce the positive and control the direction. Use your body language, such as leaning forward and nodding, to encourage the customer to continue in the conversation. Paraphrase to show that you are listening and understand what they are saying, for example 'In other words ...' and 'So you're saying ...'

Customers love to talk about what they know! If they're getting off track gently refocus them:

» 'Great, but you were saying before about x, what did you mean?

» 'Okay, but thinking about x now ...'

Building rapport and ensuring understanding is important. Communicate with participants at their level. Jargon belongs at the office.

5. EMPLOY A LOGICAL STRUCTURE

Employ a logical structure—start broad and probe deeper into interesting areas, and then narrow down into specific areas you want to explore. This is where a good discussion guide can help. (Keep in mind, a discussion guide is just that: a guide. It's not a questionnaire or survey where every question has to be asked.) Plan your discussion guide structure in advance, but be flexible. Start with the end in mind: define the business opportunity/problem so that you are clear what you are seeking knowledge for. Here is a framework for drafting your discussion guide that you can tailor to the specific opportunity space you're exploring; test it on a couple of research interviews and then iterate if need be:

» Start broad, with the broadest context being who they are, their life and work/business.

» Cover their general behaviour and their usage of broadest category (for example, finance), what products do they use and why? When and where do they purchase or consume these?

» Break apart the category your opportunity falls within and get them to talk about each part (for example, personal, corporate, small business …)

» Focus on the specific category you are exploring (for example, small business banking).

» Focus on brand and experiences of interest, and explore deeper into the experience; identify key needs, pain and delight points they have.

» Recount what you heard and check if you misinterpreted or missed anything.

» Explore your hypothesis, the concepts prepared earlier or developed in the interview.

» Ask if they have any final questions.

» To close, thank and reimburse them for their time.

6. ASK OPEN QUESTIONS

Some questions are best not asked directly—open questions will prevent dead ends. If you ask a customer 'Why do you bank with Bank X?' they're likely to provide a rational answer, for example 'convenience'. They need help to understand the true drivers (convenience is probably only one of many).

Beginning questions with 'How', 'What', 'Could you tell me about' tend to encourage customers to talk and generate their own unique answers.

Avoid leading questions or emotionally loading them. 'Do you feel most stressed using your phone when you are driving?' should be: 'How do you feel when using your phone driving?'

7. SEEK STORIES

Really engage with your end customers to learn who they are. Where possible, conduct the research while the experience is still fresh with the customer, so they are not remembering it. Otherwise, try these tips from the Institute of Design at Stanford:

» Tell me about the last time you …

» Tell me about an experience you've had with …

» How did you feel when x happened?

» What were you feeling at that moment?

8. PROBE, PROBE, PROBE

The first answer is rarely the truth. We need to probe deeper into drivers of attitude or behaviours. Dig deeper by exploring why:

» Can you tell me why that matters?

» Okay. And that is important because?

But overuse of asking 'Why?' can sound very confrontational. As you get more comfortable interviewing try alternative wording:

» How come?

» Tell me about that.

» So to clarify ...

Customers often use adjectives or descriptors. Clarify what these words mean: 'So what do you mean by x?'

Don't be afraid to challenge or question what they are saying.

9. GIVE A HELPING HAND

Customers sometimes struggle to articulate what they are thinking or feeling. While being careful not to lead, it's okay to use stimulus, summarise and prompt if necessary:

» So when you say x phrase, do you mean y or z?

» To summarise, you're saying that x has three parts. [List the parts.] Is that correct?

Don't lead customers by finishing their sentences. Always ask their permission and allow them to disagree with your ideas if you are helping them out.

Stimulus can provide ways to explore issues deeper—especially if conversation comes to a standstill.

10. TAKE NOTES

It is important to take notes during and after the interview, otherwise you will forget or distort the interview. If taking notes during the interview, don't get distracted. Go to a quiet place immediately afterward to complete your notes. Some tips for note-taking:

» Make sure you tell customers in your introduction that you will be taking notes.

» Draw pictures, write good quotes and make notes.

» Capture what you see, including the context, artefacts, the customer and their body language and actions.

» Capture what you hear, including quotes, stories, key words and contradictions. Contradictions can occur from what they say versus what they actually do.

» Capture what your customer is feeling and thinking—emotions, beliefs and confusion.

» There is no translation or interpretation at this stage. Be specific, give detail and reference the customer.

» Don't come back empty-handed—notes are your foundation for insight!

If there are three of you, you can have an interviewer, note-taker and observer—but be mindful you are not freaking the customer out!

11. BE AN OBJECTIVE SPONGE

Leave your own beliefs at the door. It's important that you don't judge customers' responses—otherwise you won't get the truth out of them.

Be an active listener. Avoid problem solving or placating customers as they speak—you won't tune into what is important.

Silence is golden. Let customers fill the silence; they should do 90 per cent of the talking!

3. DISTILLING KEY OBSERVATIONS AND FINDINGS

At the next stage you and your team (all the different pairs that did the interviews) will come back together to unpack, share and distill all your observations into needs and insights. But you can't share everything from your research word for word; you won't have time and you wouldn't want to. So it is really important before your group synthesis sessions to identify the key observations from your knowledge review and research fieldwork.

I find I work best by going to a quiet and relaxing place like a café and reading through all my notes and highlighting the most striking observations—that I saw, heard, read or experienced. It's a very qualitative and gut-feel process, so there are no hard and fast rules. When you're starting out, try looking for workarounds, surprises, anomalies, undesired outcomes, obstacles, risks, desires, tensions, contradictions and simply just things that stand out. (Use a mix of intuition and reasoning. The more you do this type of activity the better you get at it.) The final check I use is to ask myself: if I only had five to ten minutes to debrief all my findings from across each interview I did, what would be the key findings I'd share?

In this chapter I have aimed to set you and your team up to run stage 2: Discover on your own, but there is no harm in involving your research manager if you have one (we always have one on our cross-functional team) and/or a research team from an agency or consultancy. In the discovery (and testing) phase I almost always involve specialist qualitative researchers to work alongside the team. (Alongside, not instead of—it is really important that the whole team build empathy and understanding for the customer.) A good qualitative researcher lives and breathes this type of work, doing it day in day out, and can offer great advice and tips. If you and your team are new to this, attending a few discovery sessions with a qualitative researcher before going out on your own can be a great way to get up to speed quicker. If you're strapped for cash then you can run the discovery phase on your own, but even a little bit of expert help up front can make a big difference.

Another great resource to help you think about, plan and conduct successful field research is my good friend Nick Bowmast's book, *USERPALOOZA: A field researcher's guide.*

***

That is the end of the Discover stage. You and your team have immersed yourselves into your customers' world and built empathy for who they are and what is important to them. Hopefully, you are starting to form early hunches for the insights that will unlock opportunities for innovation. Next, in stage 3: Distill insights, it'll be time to start sharing and distilling these observations across your team and crafting customer insight statements that unlock opportunity and inspire new ideas.

Learnings

- Customer needs and insights come from observing and interviewing customers, not sitting in the ivory tower making them up on an empathy map.

- Empathy is at the heart of a customer-centred innovation process. How can you innovate for someone you don't have empathy for?

- Start the discovery phase by reviewing what you already know about your customer (and lapsed and non-customers) in the opportunity space you are exploring.

- Focus new research on gaps you've identified from a knowledge and research review.

- Customer insight comes from applying and connecting multiple sources of research. Try being the customer, being with the customer and learning about them from 'experts'.

- Extreme customers are a great source of insight because their experiences are often heightened, so it is easier for your team to pick up on key needs and pains.

- Take a qualitative approach to research to get the why behind customers' behaviours.

- The behaviours we adopt as innovation teams are equally as important to the skills and tools we apply when conducting customer research. Be sure to dial up your empathy behaviours.

Questions for innovators and leaders

- Who are the customers, lapsed customers and non-customers of your current products and services?

- Does everyone in your organisation regularly spend time observing and interviewing customers? If not, how could you build it into your team's day jobs and projects? If yes, how do you link it to continuous improvement and larger projects?

- How do you currently generate customer insights? Do you make them up or craft them from real customer research and empathy?

- When planning and conducting customer research, build in some extreme customers, not just the mainstream.

- How can you ensure that every innovation and design project starts with customer discovery and insight?

- Do you have in-house research expertise to champion and manage customer-centric research?

- How many resources and how much money do you currently allocate to research for your innovation projects? Is this enough to get the results successful innovation requires?

3

DISTILL INSIGHTS

In stage two, you and your team immersed yourselves in the world of the customer to explore your broad opportunity area through their lens. During stage three you'll share your experiences and start distilling and connecting observations to craft multiple specific customer-centric opportunities within your broader opportunity area.

This is possibly the hardest phase of design and innovation. You've got to take all that you know about the customer — what you've seen, heard, read and experienced — and somehow turn that into opportunities to redesign or innovate a new product, service, experience or way of working. It requires critical and intuitive thinking, interpretation, empathy, experimentation and often some incubation and time away from the challenge. It is something that many qualitative researchers (and some others) are good at, be it through genetics or experience, and the rest of us have to practise to get better. So how do you master it and come up with insights like the one that helped BBC and *Top Gear* reverse declining viewership and ratings to become the top car program on TV?

The insight was that 'blokey males who are into cars need to be entertained because they actually like the camaraderie and banter that goes with cars more than the car tech itself'. Prior to this insight, *Top Gear* had all the tech, gadgets and technical car talk, but viewership was declining. It wasn't until they realised that the need they should really be satisfying was camaraderie, banter and humour that they turned the show around.

The key to innovation success is discovering these relevant and unmet customer needs and turning them into an actionable insight. You'll find that these needs are as much emotional and social as they are functional.

Over the years I've spent tens of thousands of hours researching, refining, practising, honing and teaching insight skills on hundreds of projects across multiple industries and continents. I am going to share the key tools for generating customer insights and, just as importantly, the key thinking skills and behaviours required to get the best results.

WHAT DO I MEAN BY 'INSIGHT'?

Insight can be thought of as:

» a feeling

» a revelation

» an aha!

» the underlying 'why' behind a customer's need(s).

As insights guru Steven Melford says, 'Insight is our inspiration for innovation, a penetrating truth that unlocks opportunity and inspires action'.

From the empathy stage we have gained a lot of understanding and observations about our customers. To get to insight we go beyond understanding by asking how and why. Let's look at an example (see figure 3.1).

OBSERVATION	INSIGHT	IDEAS
Breakfast is being skipped more frequently	– I can't face food in the morning – I don't have time	– Breakfast drink – Portable breakfast

Figure 3.1: understanding to insight
Source: Adapted from Steven Melford

In this simple example we are innovating breakfast. We know from quantitative research that the number of people skipping breakfast is growing, but this isn't insightful enough for us to innovate off. While we could innovate around that fact, we don't yet know *why* people are skipping breakfast, so we are less likely to come up with a relevant and desirable solution. We want to get deeper to the 'why', as this will lead to more creative and relevant ideas. By conducting empathy research and distilling our findings we identify two different insights as to why people skip breakfast in the morning:

1. Some people skip breakfast, because they can't face food in the morning.

2. Others simply skip breakfast because they don't have time in the morning (they prioritise other things such as sleep or exercise).

These two insights give us richer understanding into the customers' problems and allow us to come up with more specific, relevant and value-added ideas that the customers are more likely to buy.

INSIGHT GENERATION METHOD

My method for generating insights, honed and refined over the years, is:

1. story tell

2. synthesise

3. prioritise

4. craft

5. test and check.

1. STORY TELL

In this first step we want to share and understand findings across the team. Split into smaller teams of four to six people, so combine two to three interview pairs. You can go either unstructured or structured when sharing and unpacking observations. The unstructured method is to unpack directly onto flip charts or butcher paper, using sticky notes and markers, without any type of framework. The more structured approach is to use one of many synthesis frameworks, such as the Empathy Map or Customer

Profile Map. (If your project is the redesign of a customer journey, then developing personas and using a Customer Journey Map are the best tools.)

Let's start with the unstructured approach first.

BLANK MAP

 TIME
60–120 minutes

 PEOPLE
Core team of 4–6

MATERIALS
A whiteboard or wall, flip chart paper and markers.

1. Create a big space on a whiteboard or wall using about four sheets of flip chart paper.

2. Each person takes turns to share their key observations from each customer they researched. Cycle through one customer at a time and keep changing storytellers after each customer to ensure everyone gets a turn.

3. Everyone else captures observations from the storyteller, using sticky notes, and populates the flip chart. As you progress you cluster and highlight patterns and themes. Keep grouping supporting observations under each theme.

4. Keep repeating steps 2 and 3 until all customers' stories are told or time has run out.

TIP

To cluster (theme) or not to cluster, that is the question. As you go through the storytelling you and your team can start to cluster and theme the observations. My key tip, though, is to watch out for a generalising or watering down of the rich observations. Even if you cluster you want to keep the themes rich and single-minded. If you're unsure, don't cluster until you get more practised.

EMPATHY MAP

TIME
60–120
minutes

PEOPLE
Core team
of 4–6

MATERIALS
A whiteboard or wall, flip chart
paper and markers.

1. Create a four-quadrant layout on a whiteboard or wall using
    four sheets of flip chart paper (see figure 3.2).

Figure 3.2: Empathy Map
Source: Adapted from David Gray

2. Each person takes turns to share their key observations from each customer they researched. Cycle through one customer at a time and change storyteller after each customer to ensure everyone gets a turn.

3. Everyone else captures observations from the storyteller using sticky notes, and populates the four areas of the map (see figure 3.2):

   – *Say:* What are the key quotes and words the customer said about the opportunity space?

   – *Do:* What customer actions and behaviours did you notice?

   – *Think:* What thoughts can you infer the customer might be thinking?

   – *Feel:* What emotions can you infer the customer might be feeling?

4. Keep repeating steps 2 and 3 until all customers' stories are told or time has run out.

TIPS

» The richest insights tend to come from the Think and Feel side of the map. Say and Do are great leads into Think and Feel.

» Colleagues should probe the storyteller on what they think the customer was thinking and feeling to reach deeper insight.

» If once you've completed your map the Think and Feel side is still light on sticky notes, go back to the left-hand side and see whether you can infer any further thoughts and feelings.

» You can infer what the customer was thinking and feeling based on your research and knowledge of the customer, but don't make stuff up.

CUSTOMER PROFILE MAP

TIME	PEOPLE	MATERIALS
30–60 minutes	Core team of 4–6	A whiteboard or wall, flip chart paper and markers.

The Customer Profile Map can be used in much the same way as the Empathy Map. You can also complete a customer profile for each target customer segment you have identified. The customer profile allows you to go from empathy straight to jobs (needs), pains and gains, so it gives the team more guidance (guard rails) for the synthesis stage. The warning with this, though, is that you may miss out on some key opportunities by skipping some of the synthesis and thinking stages. Therefore, for innovation projects I prefer to use the Empathy Map. I find the Customer Profile Map is a good entry point for less experienced teams. But try all three (starting with the Customer Profile Map then progressing to the Empathy Map and then the Blank Map) and decide for yourself.

1. Create a circle with three even sections on a whiteboard or wall using two or four sheets of flip chart paper (see figure 3.3).

2. Each person takes turns to share their key observations from each customer they researched for that segment. Cycle through one customer at a time, and keep changing storyteller after each customer to ensure everyone gets a turn.

3. Everyone else captures observations on the three areas, using sticky notes, and populates the map.

   - *Jobs:* fundamental problems customers hope to address or needs they hope to satisfy. The jobs customers 'hire' a product or service to do for them.

   - *Pains:* bad outcomes, risks and obstacles related to jobs

   - *Gains:* outcomes customers want to achieve or benefits they are seeking.

4. Keep repeating steps 2 and 3 until all customers' stories are told or time has run out.

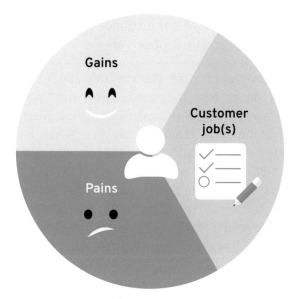

Figure 3.3: Customer Profile Map

Source: Adapted from Osterwalder, Pigneur, Bernarda, Smith, and Papadokos, *Value Proposition Design* (Hoboken, New Jersey: John Wiley & Sons, 2014)

KEYS TO STORYTELLING

The key attributes we use in the storytelling and unpacking stage are quite similar to those of the empathy research stage:

» *Empathy.* Seeing the world through the eyes of other people.

» *Beginner's eyes.* Looking at things from a fresh perspective.

» *Curiosity.* Having a sense of wonder and excitement about everything. A lust for discovery and a questioning mind.

» *Intuition.* Noticing when you react to something or not. Does it inspire you or do you feel 'so what'?

» *Objectivity.* Being aware of what you know, but being able to put this aside. Not imposing your worldview on the facts or analysis.

» *Human.* Having a conversation about your research activities (e.g. interviews) and your observations.

Once you've completed your storytelling you'll have a very full map of sticky notes and may be a little overwhelmed by the amount of data you have. Don't worry—this is quite normal. You'll be surprised at how much your brain has taken in and already started to filter. The thing to remember is that the key point of this step is to unpack and share all the team's key observations, so everyone is up to speed with each other and can marinate in all this raw data. If after completing the unpacking you still feel like you have a lot of unanswered questions about your target customers' lives and needs, then you may decide at this point to go back and do some further research to fill these gaps. Depending on how many gaps you have, I'd aim to finish one full insight cycle first, which helps you keep the momentum going, and then do extra research if still required or as part of the next cycle or project.

2. SYNTHESISE

The next step, no matter which map you used in the previous step, is to synthesise what you've unpacked. You and your team want to start pulling out the really rich and interesting observations. It's about sense making—making meaning from all these observations. This stage is a bit like the early filtering you did of your own research notes, but you now start progressing to a team (and then overall project team) view based on what the entire group uncovered and the discussions you've been having.

In saying that I prefer to start individually in your teams, so you get that entrepreneurial angle (thinking like an entrepreneur, with freedom, flexibility and passion before you become too corporate in your thinking) on it and avoid groupthink, and then progress to group sharing and iterating. The task now is to highlight the most striking observations.

EMPATHY MAP FILTER

 TIME
10–20 minutes

 PEOPLE
Core team of 4–6

 MATERIALS
Marker

1. Individually, review your team map. Look out for tensions, contradictions, surprises, workarounds, anomalies, undesired outcomes, obstacles, risks, desires and so on. Notice when you react to something or not. What are your instincts and senses telling you? Which observations inspire you or make you feel 'so what'? Selecting the ones that inspire you and ignoring the ones that make you feel 'so what?', dial up the 'keys to storytelling' from the previous section when doing this step.

2. Once you've read through the whole map, highlight the sticky notes that strike you as the most interesting by circling them or marking them with an asterisk or tick (see figure 3.4 overleaf).

TIP

The richest insights tend to come from the Think and Feel side of the Empathy Map.

Figure 3.4: Empathy Map filter

3. PRIORITISE

We're still really synthesising, but we are now synthesising and prioritising as a group. I really like Alexander Osterwalder's ranking tool, which he uses to rank jobs, pains and gains. I use it in a similar way at this stage to rank our key observations. I've named it the Opportunity Scale.

The Opportunity Scale helps you identify which observations (sticky notes) to explore first, by ranking the tensions, workarounds, desires and so on that you and your team highlighted in your map. Ranking customer tensions, workarounds and desires is helpful in selecting the needs that customers really want to see solved.

OPPORTUNITY SCALE

TIME 15–30 minutes	**PEOPLE** Core team of 4–6	**MATERIALS** A whiteboard/flip chart paper, markers and sticky notes

1. Create a scale, from important/extreme/essential at the top to insignificant/moderate/nice to have at the bottom, on flip chart paper or a whiteboard.

2. Each person takes turns to take one of their highlighted sticky notes from the map and place it on the scale relative to the other sticky notes. The team discusses the ranking, and placement, of each sticky. Also, notice when the group reacts to something or not—do the observations inspire the group, or do you feel 'so what'? Once again, dial up the 'keys to storytelling' behaviours from the last section. Repeat until all highlighted sticky notes have been placed on the scale (see figure 3.5).

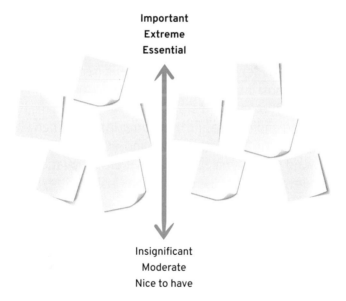

Figure 3.5: Opportunity Scale

Source: Adapted from Osterwalder, Pigneur, Bernarda, Smith, and Papadokos, *Value Proposition Design* (Hoboken, New Jersey: John Wiley & Sons, 2014)

3. The sticky notes at the top of the scale are prioritised as the first opportunities to explore.

TIPS

» When facilitating this exercise I use the analogy that at the top of the scale are things that need surgery and at the bottom they just need a bandaid. The big opportunities are the ones that need surgery. These are the problems or needs that customers care about most.

» If the group can't agree on the ranking of a sticky note, then the person who originally chose it has the final say.

4. CRAFT

Now comes the really hard part that I've been warning you about: crafting the customer problem (opportunity) statements and the key customer insight—the piece that unlocks the opportunity and inspires new ideas.

My first exposure to this, and where I really cut my teeth, was once again as a brand manager for Unilever. Unilever was, and still is, a very strong consumer insight–focused business. At Unilever you couldn't get signoff on an idea charter for a new product, brand extension, repositioning, sales promotion or communications idea without a strong and resonating consumer insight. When I was there, insight was seen as the inspiration and lifeblood for brands and innovation, and fed all marketing activities. Innovation and brand teams at Unilever not only used consumer insight, they thrived on it.

At Unilever I got to really hone and refine my skills in insight generation. What I've learned is that the process will lead to several insights, but not all insights are created equal. The ones you want to select are the ones that challenge the status quo, create the most value, are relevant and important to the customer and offer the biggest source for competitive advantage.

Insight generation is highly creative, because good insights often require connecting in a fresh and unique way separate thoughts about the industry or category you are in and the customer. They come from actually spending time with customers (as we've done) and then distilling, digging deep and connecting different observations. All of this is what makes them hard work, but when you crack an insight it is truly worth it!

You and your team will get better at insight generation with time and practice, but I also highly recommend that you include individuals in the process who are already very good at this. Seek out insightful people from your organisation and external partners to be involved in this stage.

A few years ago I got asked to be involved in developing an insight thinking skills and behaviours program to train all of Unilever's insight managers and marketers globally, so my journey has gone full circle and it was great to give back to the organisation that I learned so much from. This is how I lead and train teams to generate insights today.

CUSTOMER INSIGHT CONSTRUCT

A Customer Insight is your interpretation and framing of the customer problem or need into an opportunity statement that will inspire ideas.

Let's start by defining the construct for our customer insights. Originally I would craft three separate statements:

1. defining the customer (target customer) and the situation or context

2. articulating the need or problem the customer is trying to satisfy or solve

3. defining the insight, that distillation of their needs and why this was so important to the customer.

The context is important, because the nature of the need will be shaped by the situation.

Nowadays when I'm crafting customer insights I like to bring the three statements together as one statement or narrative, which is also how the Institute of Design at Stanford (d.school) does it. So the statement we create comprises the three elements and looks like this: CUSTOMER + NEED + INSIGHT.

The customer element is a rich and specific description of the customer(s) and often contains some description of the context, for example *a playful and active six-year-old at school*. You want the team to be able to form a picture of the customer in their mind.

The need is the obstacle/pain/desire that you've selected and refined to be worded as a relevant and important need of the customer. The most compelling needs are often emotional or social, but can be functional. Needs are necessities. Needs are distinguished from wants in that, in the case of a need, a deficiency causes a clear adverse outcome. Needs are verbs (action, state or occurrence), not nouns (solutions). Elements of the context may also be used in describing the need. For example our playful and active six-year-old **needs** *morning tea that can be eaten on the move*.

The insight is that deeper understanding of the need. They are fresh revelations about your customer and what's important to them. Insights go beyond observation by asking how and why. For example, why is it so important to the customer or so hard to solve? It really requires getting below the surface and truly understanding the motivators of your customer. Our playful and active six-year-old at school **needs** morning tea that can be eaten on the move, **because** *playing is more important at recess than sitting down and finishing your snack*. So what we have here is a tension insight. The child has to eat all her food (teacher and parents say so), but she also really wants to play with her friends. Without knowing the context we couldn't have got to this need and insight. (Now, we could have worded the insight *because being stuck sitting down and eating morning tea is boring*, but what I find that positively framed insights work best and inspire more ideas.)

You'll know when you've crafted a good customer insight statement, because it feels intuitively true and you can't help but start to think of ideas. It is what I call 'springy'. It holds the tension and intrigues people. They want to solve it. Even though I've already worked on this project, writing the customer insight statement now I want to solve it again! (I'm thinking of a lightweight tool belt that is full of snacks that can be eaten on the run …)

TIP

When running insights workshops I like to provide lots of examples and stimulus for the groups to help them with this stage. I find it gives them a kickstart and inspiration. I print out posters for each team of example needs and example customer insight statements. The posters of needs I use are from the Universal Needs as outlined by Jeanne Liedtka in her book *Designing for Growth* (see figure 3.6).

UNIVERSAL NEEDS

Connection needs
- Acceptance
- Affection
- Appreciation
- Belonging
- Cooperation
- Communication
- Closeness
- Community
- Compassion
- Consideration
- Consistency
- Empathy
- Inclusion
- Intimacy
- Love
- Mutuality
- Nurturing
- Respect
- Self-respect
- Safety
- Security
- Stability
- Support
- To know & be known
- To see & be seen
- To understand & be understood
- Trust
- Warmth

Physical needs
- Air
- Food
- Movement & exercise
- Rest and sleep
- Sexual expression
- Safety
- Shelter
- Touch
- Water

Honesty needs
- Authenticity
- Integrity
- Presence

Play needs
- Joy
- Humor

Peace needs
- Beauty
- Communion
- Ease
- Equality
- Harmony
- Inspiration
- Order

Autonomy needs
- Choice
- Freedom
- Independence
- Space
- Spontaneity

Meaning needs
- Awareness
- Celebration of life
- Challenge
- Clarity
- Competence
- Consciousness
- Contribution
- Creativity
- Discovery
- Efficacy
- Effectiveness
- Growth
- Hope
- Learning
- Mourning
- Participation
- Purpose
- Self-expression
- Stimulation
- To matter
- Understanding

Figure 3.6: Universal Needs

Source: *Designing for Growth*, Jeanne Liedtka and Tim Ogilvie, Columbia Business School Publishing, 2011

The example customer insights are a mix from projects I've worked on over the years and some I've post rationalised from well-known innovations. See if you can guess some of the products or services for the customer insights. You can use the examples here and add to them as your team and organisation progresses on its customer-centric innovation journey:

» An indulgent foodie **needs** guaranteed satisfaction, **because** if the delivered pleasure falls short of the expectation it doesn't justify the guilt.

» A young outgoing male **needs** to feel, look and smell good, **because** the dating game is a major preoccupation for him.

» A woman in her thirties who wants to look and feel her best **needs** to restore her skin, **because** using soap leaves her skin feeling dry and tight.

» A playful and active six-year-old at school **needs** morning tea that can be eaten on the move, **because** playing is more important at recess than sitting down.

» Blokey males who are into their cars **need** entertainment **because** they actually like the camaraderie and banter that goes with cars more than the car tech itself.

» A busy and confused parent **needs** to feel confident they're giving their children good nutritional choices, **because** they find it difficult with all the different health messages in the media.

Note that most of these customers are written as an individual person. This is to make it rich and specific, so you can picture the customer. It is also based on the customer or customers that the need and insight comes from. It is not meant to imply that you are only generating solutions for a universe of one.

This stage is about finding inspiration for innovation, not market validation. And inspiration often comes from depth, not breadth. While you want to keep a balance, market sizing and validation comes later, once you've uncovered something worth solving. However, if it makes you (or your organisation) more comfortable, you can frame the customer as a group with some small tweaks, for example *A playful and active six-year-old at school* can become *Playful and active primary school children*. There is more on what a good customer insight looks like in the next two steps.

START CRAFTING!

TIME 30–90 minutes	**PEOPLE** Groups of 4–6	**MATERIALS** A whiteboard/flip chart paper, markers and sticky notes

Now you're ready to start crafting your own customer insights. I like starting my teams working as individuals or pairs first and then coming together to share, refine and build. I find some quiet solo or pair thinking time first is great for this type of problem solving.

1. Working individually or in pairs, take your prioritised opportunities (sticky notes) from the Opportunity Scale. You can self select which opportunities you want to work on (probably the ones you highlighted and transferred across from the empathy map) or, depending on how many you've got, you can all work on the same ones in parallel and see what different customer insights you come up with.

2. Using a sticky note for each element—customer, need and insight—start by describing the **customer**.

   - Remember to use rich, descriptive and engaging language. Where relevant add details about the context or circumstance in the customer description and/or need.

   - Then start articulating the **need**. Really push to the emotional driver. Use the universal needs as inspiration and make sure you haven't baked a solution into it.

   - Finally, start crafting the **insight**. Do this by probing the need by continuously asking 'why' to get to the insight. For example, 'Why is the need/problem so hard to solve?' 'Why is the desire so important?' Use 'because', 'but' and 'so that' to force the interpretation.

3. Before you come back together as a team to share your customer insight statements, write each one up clearly with one sticky note for each element, but as a single customer story—not separate disconnected facts. As Clayton Christensen, author of *Competing Against Luck*, says, 'You're trying to capture the story of customers in their moments

of struggle or desire for progress'. It's still okay if you have multiple statements or stories for each opportunity; just articulate each one clearly, so they can be reviewed and iterated as a team. For example:

- *Version 1:* A playful and active six-year-old at school **needs** morning tea that can be eaten on the move, **because** playing is more important at recess than sitting down.

- *Version 2:* A playful and active six-year-old at school **needs** morning tea that can be eaten on the move, **because** being stuck sitting down and eating morning tea is boring.

- *Version 3:* A playful and active six-year-old at school **needs** morning tea that can be eaten on the move, **because** she'll be teased if she doesn't come and play until she has finished eating.

- *Version 4:* A playful and active six-year-old at school **needs** morning tea that can be eaten quickly, **because** playing with her friends is more fun than sitting and finishing her food.

4. Once you come back together as a group you want to create three columns on flip chart paper or a whiteboard with three headings—customers, needs, insights.

5. Everyone should have completed multiple sets of customer insight statements and you start sharing them by taking turns to present them back to the group while sticking them up on the flip chart or whiteboard. This is a great opportunity for everyone to build on each other's statements. I find having someone fresh listen to your statement and then summarise it back works well to really help hone and refine it (making sure to capture it on sticky notes).

***

Often when we are running a workshop or training teams this is the last exercise of the day and everyone is mentally and physically tired from a full day of activity and using their brains in a different way. As Jason Bourne says, 'Sleep is a weapon!' So we send everyone home and tell them to come back fresh in the morning and relook at and refine their customer insights.

My team and I will often come in early the next day and refine and hone their statements by applying a fresh perspective and a recharged mind. We simply tell the participants that the insight fairies have been in and we talk them through the suggested tweaks and explain how we got to them. So depending on where you are at on your innovation project it is definitely worth:

» taking a break (whether it's over lunch or overnight) and coming back fresh to your statements

» bringing someone fresh in who is also skilled in insights to offer some suggestions.

TIPS

» Each opportunity can have multiple customer insight statements. Likewise, each customer can have multiple needs and a need can have multiple insights. So when you are crafting them be creative and play with them. Generate lots of different descriptions of your customer, needs and insights, writing them all on separate sticky notes and moving them around. Sometimes you'll find you've got the order wrong or your insight is in fact a need. If that's the case move the insight to the top, making it your new need, and then try coming up with a new insight for this.

» Make the Customer Insight focused, but don't narrow the possibilities too much.

» Don't put the solution in the Customer Insight. It should inspire ideas, but not contain them.

» Write the Customer Insight in a positive sense.

» Make it inspiring. It should create passion and excitement.

» You'll know when you've crafted a good customer insight statement, because you can't help but start to think of ideas. It is what we call 'springy'. It holds tension and intrigues people; they want to solve it.

The Insights Crafting process (see figure 3.7) captures the key steps and tips to crafting good customer insight statements.

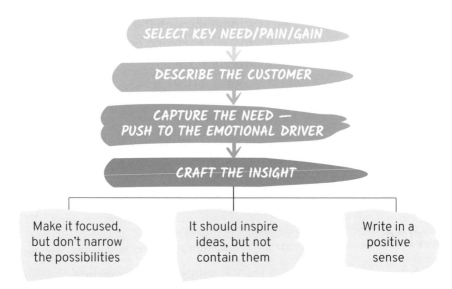

Figure 3.7: Insights Crafting process

ATTRIBUTES

We keep using the attributes of empathy, beginner's eyes, curiosity, intuition, objectivity and human. We also add:

» *playfulness.* Enjoying it and going with the process helps you get to fresh and unique insights

» *creativity.* Suspend judgement and understand and build on the insights of yourself and others.

The next step is to sense check and then select the customer insights you'd like to progress.

5. TEST AND CHECK

Now it's time to select the customer insights that you want to take forward into idea generation. The following tools can help you judge whether you have discovered a Customer Insight that inspires action and can be applied to unlock growth.

CUSTOMER INSIGHT TEST

TIME 15–30 minutes	**PEOPLE** Groups of 4–6	**MATERIALS** A whiteboard/flip chart paper, markers and sticky notes

In your teams try this simple prefix, suffix test by Steven Melford.
'Isn't it interesting that ...'

Insert your proposed customer insight statement here.

'... and as a result my initial ideas are ...'

Insert first ideas here.

If your insight statement is neither interesting nor stimulating some ideas, chances are it is not an insight, it is only a fact.

CUSTOMER INSIGHT CHECK

In your teams put your customer insight statements through the following checks:

» *Clear.* Is it clear, understandable?

» *Deep and true.* Is it a deep understanding about a customer motivation that rings true?

» *Recurring.* Is it a recurring need, not a one-off or discrete event?

» *Compelling.* Is it relevant and important to the customer?

» *Refreshing.* Does it change the way you see things?

» *Passion.* Does it create passion and excitement?

» *Actionable.* Could it lead to new business opportunities?

If your customer insight statement doesn't tick all the boxes it may need more crafting or it isn't an insight.

AN EXAMPLE INSIGHT GENERATION WORKSHOP PLAN

Table 3.1 is an example one-day insight generation workshop agenda.

Table 3.1: example one-day insight generation workshop agenda

TIMING	ACTIVITY	PURPOSE
8.30 am	**Arrival tea & coffee**	Good hospitality. Networking. Allows everyone time to prepare mentally and physically. Ensures you start on time.
9.00 am	**Welcome, introductions and objectives** Facilitators welcome the participants. Project leader sets up the project challenge and objectives of the day in an inspiring way. Facilitator breaks the group into teams. Tools: energisers	To introduce participants and teams. Creates welcoming atmosphere. Puts everyone at ease. Participants have a common vision of what success looks like and are feeling inspired.
9.30 am	**Story tell—unpack** Teams share and unpack observations from their customer activities creating a structured or unstructured customer Empathy Map. Tools: customer Empathy Map or journey	To share observations and findings across the team, so everyone has a rich understanding of each other's customer discovery experiences. Initial categorising of observations, e.g. into say, do, think and feel.
11.00 am	**Morning break**	To refresh, refuel and recharge

TIMING	ACTIVITY	PURPOSE
11.15 am	**Synthesis** Teams start distilling their observations down to the most striking. Tools: synthesise within the customer maps created earlier	To synthesise all the observations and findings into a smaller group of the most interesting and striking observations.
12.00 pm	**Prioritise** Teams rank and select the most important, extreme and essential needs, pains etc. Tool: Opportunity Scale	To make choices on what observations to progress based on what we know about the customer and what we believe is most important to them.
12.30 pm	**Lunch**	To refresh, refuel, recharge and reflect
1.15 pm	**Craft** Teams craft their prioritised observations into customer insight statements. Tools: Customer Insight Construct	To craft a set of customer insight statements that inspire and unlock opportunity.
3.15 pm	**Afternoon break**	To refresh, refuel, recharge and reflect
3.30 pm	**Test and check** Teams now review and select the customer insight statements they want to take forward into idea generation.	To ensure you are focusing your idea generation on customer insights that inspire action and unlock growth.

(continued)

Table 3.1: example one-day insight generation workshop agenda (*cont'd*)

TIMING	ACTIVITY	PURPOSE
4.30 pm	**Showcase and next steps** Teams share back their selected customer insights. Project leader discusses actions and next steps. Tools: Insights gallery (where you showcase your insight statements to the other teams)	To give everyone the chance to see all the customer insights generated across the different teams. To keep momentum up, ensures everyone is clear about next steps and opportunities to stay involved.

These tools, and your increasing experience over time, help you sort through and select the best customer insights to take forward into idea generation. How many you select depends on how much time, people, energy and money you have to explore and develop them. If I'm running a one-day idea generation workshop next I like to have four teams (more on this in stage 4: Ideate). And I find each team can ideate on two to three customer insights before they become a bit mentally stale and need a decent break (overnight or for a few days). So you are looking at taking between eight and twelve customer insight statements forward for this type of ideation workshop, but, as you'll find in the next stage, ideation and brainstorming can be run in many different ways.

You've completed the hardest part (in my view) of the design and innovation journey. You've distilled what is important to your customers and crafted opportunity statements that can become springboards for idea generation. Next, in stage 4a: Ideate: Incubate & create, I'll share some creative new ways for incubating and generating ideas to solve these customer insights.

Learnings

- The quality of insight you generate is directly linked to the quality and depth of the previous discovery phase.

- Customer insights are not data or observations. They require synthesising and connecting and go beyond understanding by asking how and why.

- Insight generation in my opinion is the hardest phase of the front end of innovation. It is a craft that takes practice and guidance from experts.

- Insights come from storytelling, synthesising, connecting, prioritising, crafting, testing and checking.

- The insight phase distils and then frames the customer need and pains we observed in the field into opportunity statements that will inspire ideas.

- These opportunity statements are framed as customer narratives called customer insights. They consist of a description of the customer and the context or situation, the need they want to satisfy and the insight to why the need is so important or hard to solve.

- You'll often know when you've crafted a good customer insight, because you can't help but to start thinking of ideas and solutions.

- Good insight generation requires a break away from the task to reflect and get fresh eyes.

- Use an experienced insight facilitator to provide expert direction and fresh eyes.

- Keep using your empathy behaviours from the discovery phase, plus dial up your playfulness and creativity.

Questions for innovators and leaders

- How might you ensure every innovation brief (and other business activities) has a signed-off important and unmet customer need and insight?

- How skilled are your teams in insight generation? Do you have a critical number of practitioners?

- As a leader do you role model the importance and value of customer insights and use them to craft real customer research?

- Do you showcase great (and not so great) insights and the innovation initiatives they led to, so people can continually learn and evolve?

- Are you applying insight to the improvement of your people (employee) experience too?

4^A

IDEATE

INCUBATE
& CREATE

In stage three, you and your team shared your customer immersion experiences, distilled what is important to your customers, and crafted opportunity statements that can be leveraged as springboards for idea generation. In stage 4a, you'll incubate and work on boosting your team's creative confidence ready for generating fresh new ideas.

From my experience if you've got great customer insights then you can't help but come up with exciting new ideas for solving your customers' problems. However, you can increase the quantity and quality of your ideas further by increasing your creativity and applying it to idea generation.

Edward de Bono has done much to demystify creativity and inspire many of us to rediscover our own creativity. De Bono emphatically states that without creativity there are no ideas, and without ideas organisations and the people within them will stagnate and neither will reach any sort of fulfilment. This is really important to me. We spend so much of our lives at work, so we want work to be as fulfilling as possible. Creativity plays a key role in providing this meaning and fulfilment. And it goes without saying that we need creativity to design and innovate.

We also know from the author of *Flow*, Mihaly Csikszentmihalyi, that human beings are at their happiest (in flow, or 'the zone') when they are creating. People actually long to express their creativity and in this chapter I'll share with you how to unleash it.

INCUBATION

Coming up with really good ideas can be quite an unpredictable process. We can increase our chances by first of all incubating and tapping into our subconscious. There is plenty of scientific evidence that highlights the importance of the subconscious in generating ideas. For example, as Baroness Susan Greenfield, a British scientist and member of the House of Lords, has observed, many people feel they have their best ideas in the shower, out walking or on holidays. But it's not the holiday itself that is conducive to creating ideas, but rather that it's providing a silent, non-distracting, non-reactive environment. Being in a place where time has slowed down to a non-fire-fighting pace is great for incubating. So before you jump straight into ideas or running brainstorms, it's well worth giving your teams some time to incubate first around the problems (customer insights) you are solving.

As Mihaly Csikszentmihalyi defines it,

> Incubation is when you allow a problem to churn around below the threshold of consciousness ... And the longer you allow, it seems, the bigger the breakthrough is ... Incubation time leads to Eurekas. Cognitive theorists believe that ideas, when deprived of conscious direction, follow simple laws of association. They combine more or less randomly, forming new ideas.

So how do we incubate? Well, according to Professor Richard Wiseman, author of best-selling books *The Luck Factor* and *Did You Spot the Gorilla?*, 'Given that so much of the process seems to take place in an unconscious, and somewhat mysterious, way, I suspect that such a formula will forever be beyond our grasp'. However, from the research and ideas of many like Wiseman and Csikszentmihalyi we can indeed come up with a kind of formula, even if it hasn't been scientifically proven yet.

Based on research and my experience in creativity and innovation, I find that the following steps work really well:

1. Build a firm understanding of the problem (Discover and Distill insights stages).
2. Prime your brain (with the problem to be solved).
3. Get into a creative or incubative state and jot down any ideas.

1. BUILD A FIRM UNDERSTANDING OF THE PROBLEM

This is what you've been doing in the Discover and Distill insights stages — building a firm understanding of the customer, who they are and what unmet needs they have.

2. PRIME YOUR BRAIN

According to Wiseman, 'People who have good ideas are skilled at priming themselves with a particular problem and therefore spotting the solution to that problem, or something that will lead them to a solution, when it happens to pop up in front of them'. To demonstrate what we mean by priming, try this exercise from Wiseman:

1. Have a quick look around the room or space you are in now, making a mental note of what you see.

2. Now choose one of these four colours: red, blue, green or yellow.

3. Look around again, but this time focus on any objects that match your chosen colour.

Most people note that they noticed different things the second time around. This is because you calibrated your brain to recognise the things you missed the first time. And this can be the same for creativity. By priming our brains with a customer problem our brains will start subconsciously looking for solutions for it.

3. GET INTO A CREATIVE OR INCUBATIVE STATE

How you are at any given moment is your state. Chris Barez-Brown says you can think of your state as how you are feeling emotionally, physically, mentally and spiritually. Chris is very passionate about the role of state in creativity and innovation and has done lots of research and run many experiments in this space to test out his thinking, which you can learn more about in his book *How to Have Kick-Ass Ideas*. Chris would always say 'it is not just what you do, but how you do it'. Combine the doing of creativity with the being.

Professor Richard Wiseman provides another way to think about our state, by looking at our brain wave frequencies (shown in figure 4a.1):

» Beta is when we are awake and focused, like at work; it is our dominant state.

» Alpha is a deep relaxation. Relaxed, yet still alert.

» Theta is our subconscious (dreaming, deep meditation).

» Delta is deep sleep.

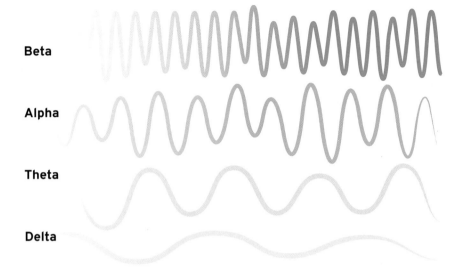

Beta

Alpha

Theta

Delta

Figure 4a.1: brain wave frequencies

When we are incubating ideas we want to get into alpha or theta. Professor Wiseman says that when Thomas Edison was trying to solve problems he would sit on a chair in a large metal dish holding a heavy object in his hands, like a stone. He'd then relax and try to get into theta to tap into his subconscious to solve the problem he was working on. If he relaxed too much and went into deep sleep (delta) the stone would drop—bang! The loud noise would wake him up and he'd start the process over again. While you don't have to go to this much effort to set up a mechanism for tapping into your subconscious, it is important to build time for incubation in your projects. Here are some more practical ways to get into an incubative or subconscious state.

TIME AND SPACE

You need to give yourself time and space to incubate and have ideas. Chasing a deadline or hurriedly writing a report or presentation at your desk won't encourage your best ideas. This is beta state activity and is great for getting stuff done, but ideas don't come from thinking hard!

Baroness Susan Greenfield recommends starting by finding a quiet space (although white noise can be okay, like in a café) where you can work uninterrupted—a place where time has slowed to a non-fire-fighting mode. Then create physical space in your immediate vicinity (e.g. clear the table you are working at). Then start with a blank piece of paper, where you can work unencumbered by any boundaries or framework. And just doodle. As Greenfield says,

> What helps to preserve and develop individuality and hence enhance creativity ... where it is easy to forget the outside world and concentrate completely on the task at hand ... a setting in which you can work on the problems that intrinsically motivate you, that allows easy and uninterrupted concentration.

LETTING GO—BEING YOUR TRUE SELF

A few years ago I did some work with Giles Foreman at Central St Martins College in London. Giles is a coach for actors, and a very good one—he's trained many Hollywood stars in the creative arts and method acting. When Giles is running you through your paces he encourages you to let go, just be your true self and to use your imagination, as you need to use your imagination to be creative.

This explains why many people are more creative in their lives outside work. Sometimes in public or at work we wear a 'mask' to protect ourselves by not sharing our full self. However, to be truly creative we need to remove this mask and turn up as our true selves. At the beginning of class Giles would take us through exercises to allow our whole body and mind to let go. We'd start by relaxing our bodies, warming them up and releasing any tension. Then we'd move onto the mind, clearing the worries and dead wood that block the creative pathways and consume space and thoughts in our mind. As Giles says, 'When you forget yourself, something comes out.'

SEMI-AUTOMATIC ACTIVITIES

Another way to allow your subconscious to start working is by doing some kind of semi-automatic activity. As Mihaly Csikszentmihalyi notes, this is an activity that only 'takes up a certain amount of attention while leaving some of it free to make connections among ideas below the threshold of conscious intentionality'. Everyday activities like having a shower, going for a run or walk, doing the dishes or preparing vegetables for dinner are all examples of semi-automatic activities.

INSPIRING ENVIRONMENTS

Visiting unusual and beautiful surroundings can have a number of effects. They:

» assist in changing our perspective to see situations from more complete and unique viewpoints

» jolt our attention out of its regular patterns and entice to try more unique and interesting paths

MORNING DIARIES

Julia Cameron, the author of *The Artist's Way*, shares her experiences of how she overcame her creative blocks to be creative again. One of the techniques she used was something she called Morning Diaries. Every morning, as soon as she woke, she would write three pages of whatever was in her mind. Just dump it down. The idea being that this clears the worries and dead wood that block the creative pathways and consume space and thoughts in your mind, thus freeing up space for fresh ideas, just as letting go of yourself does.

ARTIST'S DATES

Another technique by Julia Cameron, and complementary to inspiring environments, is taking your muse (self) on Artist's Dates. By exploring new places and objects our brains collect inspiration for new ideas. As Professor Richard Wiseman says, 'If you always focus in the same place you are limiting the material that your primed mind has to work with'.

When are you at your creative best or in your creative zone? What are your triggers to getting into a creative state? You can help identify what has worked best for you in the past by answering the following questions:

1. When do you have your best ideas (for example, what time of the day, day of the week)?

2. Where do you have your best ideas (for example, in the shower, in the park, at work, in a bar, at the library)?

3. Who do you have your best ideas with (for example, on your own, with a number of people, with particular people)?

4. What are you doing when you have your best ideas (for example, eating, socialising, walking, reading)?

CREATIVE BRIEFS

Kickstart and inspire your team's incubation and creativity by designing some creative briefs first. A creative brief is an area of focus and inspiration for incubation and idea generation that is derived from your customer insights — usually one creative brief per customer insight. Think of them as a springboard for idea generation.

Each creative brief has:

1. a headline (imagine what you'd write on a placard for a protest march for your customer insight)

2. context that sets the scene and gives some explanation to the situation

3. the customer insight

4. a number of 'how might we' questions to provide different ways in to the solution.

Here's an example.

» *Headline*: Eat on the Run

» *Context*: Primary school children have 15 minutes for recess and they must sit down to eat their food in the first five minutes. But most primary school-aged children are too small to finish a whole snack like an apple in five minutes. If they are still sitting there finishing it after five minutes then they are missing out on serious playtime with their friends and can even be teased for this.

» *Customer insight*: A playful and active six-year-old at school **needs** morning tea that can be eaten on the move, **because** playing is more important at recess than sitting down.

» How might we:

   − make snacks that can be eaten on the run?

   − make snacks that can be eaten with one hand?

   − make snacks that are quicker to eat?

   − make snacks that are portable?

   − combine eating and play time at recess?

You then circulate these to your team before incubation and ideation. They are also a great way to get others outside involved in the project. You can share them with as many people as you want and get them to send their ideas back into a central resource that you can review before your ideas workshop or, alternatively, take them forward into your ideation workshops and review there. You can even put them on a crowdsource platform and get ideas from across your whole organisation or even the world. When I was working in the London HQ of a global brand and innovation agency we actually set up a creative panel for the crowdsourcing of ideas. This panel consisted of talented creative thinkers from all walks of life, providing us with a diverse set of minds and ideas.

APPLYING INCUBATION FOR INNOVATION

Start by sending the creative briefs out to the teams in advance of your idea generation workshops — either give each team a full set or just the one to three they'll work on in the ideation workshops. Set yourself and your team the task of being their true selves, letting go and having fun or finding a space where they can do this.

Then, either individually or collectively, choose some of the incubation activities above, such as going for a walk in an inspiring environment or visiting stores from a totally different category. You can even design set activities for each creative brief and/or a day out of the office for your team to go on a creative safari like this one we did for Sainsbury's in London quite a few years ago.

We were working for Sainsbury's on their produce and bakery categories. The brief was all about helping them be better known for freshness in these categories. So we designed a day out of the office for ourselves and the Sainsbury team. We prepared for the day by doing some desk research on the internet, exploring places around London that did 'freshness' really well. Places such as florists, fresh food delis, bakers, fishmongers, even day spas. We then created safari packs for each team, which included a list of places to visit including directions on how to get there plus a London tube map. We all met up in London bright and early in the morning and headed out to track down and explore our target locations.

At the fishmonger's we got talking to them about freshness — what freshness meant to them and how did they 'do fresh'? They started telling us about how they only bought their fish fresh from day boats. 'What is a day boat?' was our next question. They explained that day boats go out each morning and come back every night with their fresh catch, whereas other boats go out for longer (several days or weeks at a time) and have big freezers on board where they freeze their catch. So by only buying from day boats the fishmonger was able to sell the freshest fish possible. So we wondered, What if Sainsbury's baked their bread fresh every day and sourced their ingredients from within a day's travel? They could then promote this to their shoppers and it would be a good way of supporting their positioning around freshness. Nowadays all supermarkets bake their bread daily and food miles has become a big trend, but at the time it was a great way of differentiating themselves in the market and building their story around freshness.

TIP

Remind team members they are to jot down all ideas they have during their incubation activities, no matter how unformed they are. A simple way to do this is to provide each team member with an inspiration template like figure 4a.2.

Write your user insight

Active and healthy working father of three needs to find fresh natural products, because when it comes to food he trusts Mother Nature best.

Stimulus	Their solution	New ideas
e.g. person, shop, industry	How they solve for this type of need/insight	for solving your Customer Insight
Fishmonger	*The fishmonger solves for freshness by only sourcing fish from day boats.*	· *Bread that is baked and delivered daily* · *Bread with batch numbers* · *Fresh, home-delivered bread* · *Bread-baking van like mobile crêpe, ice-cream or coffee van* · *Bread made only from locally-sourced ingredients*

Figure 4a.2: inspiration framework

BOOSTING CREATIVITY

You've probably already come to the conclusion that creativity and the ability to generate ideas doesn't have to be purely random or serendipitous. I'd like to add that it's also not just a gift some of us are lucky to be born with, nor is it purely the domain of the creative department. Edward de Bono has demonstrated through practical techniques it is a 'thinking skill that can be learnt' and 'those who develop the most skill will be more creative'. A key to creative thinking is generating and using inspiration and provocation to stimulate new ideas—what de Bono terms 'lateral thinking'. This stimulus is your inspiration and raw material for creativity and ideas.

Your brain needs to be primed with a specific problem that needs solving, and then given stimulus and space in order to allow new ideas to surface. In **stage 4b: Idea generation workshops** I'll show you how to plan for and make ideas happen.

But before I start teaching specific idea generation techniques it is worth understanding the key blockers that will get in the way of any individual, team or organisation's creativity, no matter how good the creative exercises in a workshop are. There are at least five key blockers to individual and team creativity:

1. beliefs
2. behaviours
3. the brain
4. state
5. space.

It is really important when you are setting up your ideas phase, workshop, room and/or lab that you design it to overcome these common barriers.

CREATIVITY BLOCKER 1: BELIEFS

If you ask a group of people in a room to put up their hand if they are creative, you'll get a couple of tentative arms raised. Ask a group of six-year-olds in a classroom and they'll all put their hands up. So what happens between age six and adulthood? We seem to go through school, society and our working lives having our creativity taught out of us. As Pablo Picasso summed it up, 'Every child is an artist. The problem is how to remain an artist when [we grow] up.'

I've worked with tens of thousands of people, hundreds of teams and organisations to help them rediscover this creative talent. What I find works best, what builds back that belief in one's own creativity, is experiences—experiences being creative and generating ideas. We teach people the tools and give them an experience using them and they see the increase in their creative capacity and in turn build creative confidence. So we work on beliefs indirectly.

When kicking off an ideas session I'll start by reminding people how creative they were as children and that 'today we are going to harness that inner child and rediscover and unleash your hidden creativity'. I share how it takes a multidisciplinary team effort to redesign or create a new innovation, and that anything else is a myth, as Anne Miller, director of the Creativity Partnership, says:

> Too often people deem themselves non-creative because they fail to live up to the unrealistic myth that true innovators generate brilliant, radically different, fully formed ideas. Breaking free from this myth is the first step in realising one's creative potential.

I then like to touch on the work by Edward de Bono and how he has taught people all around the world to be more creative through his lateral thinking techniques. Because, as de Bono says, when creativity is regarded as a magic gift, there is nothing that can be done about it. But everyone can develop some skill in lateral thinking and those who develop the most skill will be most creative.

One quick exercise I do like to do to show people their latent creative capacity is a little improvisation exercise. I get everyone to stand together in a circle and tell them that we are going to create a story, just for fun, and that anything goes. You kick off the story by making something up, for example 'I was walking home from work late one night and then …' After the 'and then' you 'pass' the story on to the next person. So they continue: 'And then I heard a noise from behind a rubbish bin, and then …' And so the story continues. I then debrief the key lessons:

1. When they lower the stakes, put aside their disbelief and have fun, they all come up with creative story lines.

2. The story got more and more creative when they built on each other's storyline.

Creativity is about having original thoughts and ideas, but we can't do this if we believe ourselves incapable of having ideas and thinking creatively—it becomes a self-fulfilling prophecy.

CREATIVITY BLOCKER 2: BEHAVIOURS

Our everyday business behaviour is not conducive to creativity. It's been refined over the years to help us in a fast-paced world where swift analysis and making fast decisions based on sound evidence is king. It involves elements of criticism and relies on critical reasoning skills when we are assessing one idea or recommendation versus another. This mode of thinking dates all the way back to the Greek philosophers and how they would use critical debate to 'prove' their theories. It's not that this approach is wrong, it's just not right for creativity.

At this stage of the innovation journey an idea can be killed by a yawn, a laugh, a comment like 'we've tried that before' or some other form of judgement. At this stage in idea generation the ideas are still just seedlings and aren't ready for harvesting (judging). We need to build on them further before we can confidently judge which are the good and bad ideas.

So when you are going into a creative phase, for example, an ideas workshop, you need to ask everyone to suspend their typical business-world behaviours and take these steps to promote creativity:

1. suspend your judgement
2. understand each other's ideas
3. build on each other's ideas.

Building on ideas is critical to this stage and innovation. Transplanting and cross-fertilising ideas from one brain to another helps create breakthrough, not incremental ideas. These days most people are quite familiar with the 'no judging' rule in brainstorming, so you shouldn't have too many problems, but it is still important to start by setting up the ground rules.

CREATIVITY BLOCKER 3: THE BRAIN

Our brain is another barrier to creativity. Most of us naturally think in a linear and analytical way. This is because the brain is a massive self-organising storage device, like all the folders on your desktop or shared drive. It's a place where logic presides (well, maybe not like everyone's desktop).

So when you ask your brain to think of an idea, say a new type of ice cream, then it immediately goes into its file on ice cream. And what does it find in there? All the experiences you've had with regard to ice cream — in a cone, in cups, in bowls for dessert, with lemonade to make a spider and so on. And none of it is new thinking. This is the very thing Einstein was talking about when he said 'Problems cannot be solved by thinking within the framework in which they were created'.

What you have to do is 'trick' your brain to go to a different file and find some different stimulus to inspire new ideas. For example, a problem with ice cream is that on a hot day the warmth from the sun melts it too quickly.

Question for a different part of the brain: What else keeps things colder for longer? Answer: a beer bottle cooler. Idea: what if we could make a beer bottle cooler for ice cream?

Now, this might not turn out to be a great idea, but you can see how we get more novel ideas by tricking (stimulating) the brain to think differently by accessing a different file. This is Edward de Bono's 'lateral thinking' again.

Creativity requires lateral thinking. Lateral thinking gets you new stimulus to solve your challenge. What I mean by 'stimulus' is anything that acts as inspiration, stimulation or provocation to think of new ideas. It can come from prior experiences stored in a different part of your mind (like the beer cooler), new experiences where you go out and search for fresh stimulus (like the Sainsbury's creative safari) and creative thinking exercises, which I'll provide later in stage 4b: Idea generation workshops. When planning your ideas phase and/or workshops you need to create this stimulus prior to the sessions. Think of it as the raw material for the ideation phase.

CREATIVITY BLOCKER 4: STATE

We touched on state earlier in this chapter, and, as mentioned, it is covered in more depth in the fabulous book *How to Have Kick-Ass Ideas*. But for now, it's worth reminding you that getting yourself and your team in the right state for the incubation step is just as important for the ideas step. As the project leader or facilitator you need to design the ideas sessions to help people get into the right creative behaviours and state. You can have the best creative briefs and exercises in the world, but if the team isn't connected then it won't happen: there'll be no magic.

So when designing your ideas session, think about what is going to get people in the right state emotionally, physically, mentally and spiritually. And what barriers are going to get in the way of this. Have you got people who have to drop kids off beforehand, so they'll be late and distracted? Have you got people who are going to be ducking in and out for meetings? Have some of the team got an important deadline due for another project? Has everyone bought into the objectives? Will there be plenty of food, refreshments and breaks? How is the room set up? Is it comfortable and relaxing?

Chris Barez-Brown, founder of consultancy Upping Your Elvis and best-selling author, shares in figure 4a.3 what it feels like when your state is stuck and ideas are impossible.

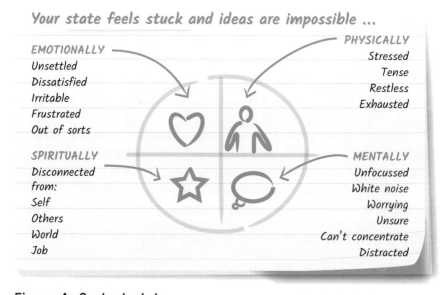

Figure 4a.3: stuck state
Source: Chris Barez-Brown, *How to Have Kick-Ass Ideas*, 2006

And figure 4a.4 shows what your state might look like when it is ready for creativity.

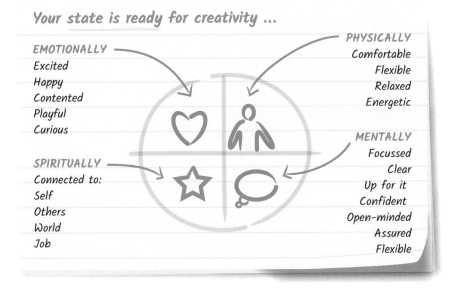

Figure 4a.4: creative state
Source: Chris Barez-Brown, *How to Have Kick-Ass Ideas*, 2006

Check in with your state now, as practice. How does your body feel? What emotions do you feel? What's going on in your head? How do you feel spiritually?

Try keeping a log of what triggers put you and your teams in a good or bad state for creativity. Over time you'll create a surefire design brief for the perfect ideation workshops. And don't forget about the steps to get into an incubative state mentioned earlier in this chapter.

CREATIVITY BLOCKER 5: SPACE

One of the biggest triggers to state and our creativity is the environment or space we are in. Mihaly Csikszentmihalyi actually believes 'it is easier to enhance creativity by changing conditions in the environment than by trying to make people think more creatively'. Well, what if we could combine the learnings of Csikszentmihalyi and de Bono?

Like our behaviours at work, our actual workplace is often designed for the business world and not the creative world. Many workplaces (even modern ones) are based on the old sweat shops, where we are lined up in rows of desks set up to enable us to work quickly and efficiently, dealing with administrative tasks and out-of-control inboxes. They are very out*put*, not out*come* focused, open plan and interrupted. Great for getting tasks done, but not that conducive to the ideas stage of the innovation journey!

What does a space for creativity and ideas look like? Having run literally thousands of ideation workshops around the world in some fantastic venues (and some pretty awful ones) I can confidently share with you what works and what doesn't. Here is a bit of a checklist of what you should be designing into your creative spaces:

» Lots of natural light. Mushrooms might grow in the dark, but ideas won't.

» Layout and furniture needs to encourage creativity, collaboration, action and design doing.

» Comfortable seating that relaxes everyone. (Although in my workshops we are standing most of the time, working on whiteboards or butcher-papered walls, so try to avoid having too many tables and chairs in the room. I get people to stand, because our state is more energised standing than sitting.)

» Lots of large whiteboards, whiteboard walls or blank walls for your exercises.

» Designated prototyping kit and a space to create prototypes. (When I visited San Francisco and Silicon Valley with New Zealand Trade and Enterprise organisation Better by Design a few years ago, every company we visited had designated prototyping spaces where teams could access the tools and materials to make quick, cheap, good-enough mock-ups of their solutions.)

» Signal that failure is okay. Some innovation labs I've visited or worked in are just too pristine and designed more as client showrooms. (What I love about d.school's space is it is designed to signal that failure is okay. Jeremy Utley and Perry Klebahn from d.school talk about how you could knock over a pail of paint and it would be fine.) Think about what signals your space is sending. Are we creating an environment where there is no judging and anything goes? And remember the front end of innovation is messy, so allow for and expect this.

» Food is important to keep people fuelled, but also signals that one is partly socialising. A meeting with food is more human!

» Music is a great mood lifter, state changer and facilitation tool.

» Tech needed for slides, videos, music or anything else. People have different learning styles—a mix of visual, auditory, written and kinaesthetic—and not everyone is the same, so keep mixing it up.

A couple of other great resources to help you boost yours and your team's creativity are *Sticky Wisdom: How to start a creative revolution at work* by ?WhatIf! This book is a classic and inspired me as a brand manager all those years back. And more recently, *Creative Confidence: Unleashing the creative potential within us all* by Tom and David Kelley

***

Right, you've now got a firm understanding of the customer problem, you've primed your brain and you've got into a creative and incubative state. Your subconscious is bursting with forming ideas, so it's time to start sharing them out with your team. It's time to start idea generation!

4B

IDEATE

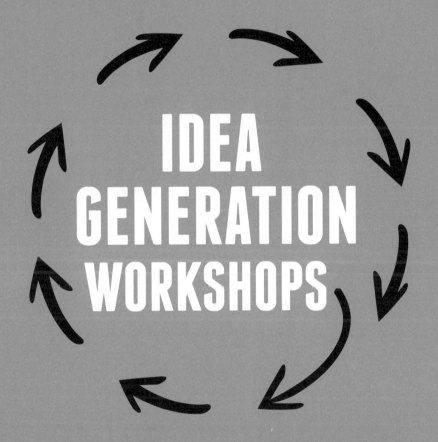

IDEA
GENERATION
WORKSHOPS

In stage 4a, you incubated on your creative briefs and boosted your teams creative confidence. In stage 4b, you will get creative to generate multiple possible solutions for your creative briefs. You'll then harvest these down and flesh them out into prototyping briefs to take into the experimentation stage.

Your team is all set now for the actual generation of ideas. They have the belief, the right behaviours, are in the right state and space. Now I'll take you through some approaches for stimulating creative thinking and generating ideas.

PREPARE

In preparation for your idea generation session you'll want to complete the following steps.

1. INVOLVE THE RIGHT PEOPLE AT THE RIGHT TIME

You'll want to find a multidisciplinary team of idea generators and idea developers. The most innovative organisations in the world, such as Gore, 3M and Unilever, work in cross-functional innovation teams, not silos with handovers between departments. Get your designers and developers involved too. Not only will they have different ideas, but it is also great for buy-in to the ideas that you'll be asking them to design and build later on.

Avoid any negative people for the ideation steps. You can always bring them in for the judging or stress-testing steps. The same can apply to senior management too, if you think they are going to stop people from thinking really creatively or if they are going to be disruptive by popping in and out. Use people where they fit best and can play a positive role. The rest can be engaged by getting them to submit ideas prior to the workshop through the creative briefs and/or to review ideas and concepts afterwards.

Most workshop venues can fit four teams. The ideal team size for brainstorming is six, plus or minus two. Any more than that and not everyone gets enough time to contribute, or people can hide. Any less and you haven't got enough diversity and people to bounce ideas off. So you are looking at an overall workshop size of 16 to 32, plus facilitators, visualisers and any other shared resources.

2. CIRCULATE THE CREATIVE BRIEFS

Circulate the briefs to all the attendees one to two weeks prior to the workshop to allow enough incubation time, encouraging them to read them as early as possible. (Mihaly Csikszentmihalyi identified that the longer the incubation time, the better the ideas.) You can even give them some set incubation activities to do (see the earlier section on incubation in this chapter). If you're running a multi-day design/innovation sprint with back-to-back days, then build in some incubation time and activities, like a creative safari between the insights day/session and the ideas day/session. Multi-day back-to-back sprints risk becoming more about theatre and efficiency than quality and true innovation without these types of natural pauses. Include a brief background blurb on the project and all the logistical details such as time, date, place. Here's an example introduction:

We are working together with teams A and B on Project X with the objective of Y. The focus to date has been on building empathy for our customers in this space — understanding who they are, what is important to them (their needs), what pains them and what delights them.

We are now moving to the generation of ideas to solve these customer needs, pains and gains. And this is why we've enlisted you and your creative skills for the ideation workshop.

The following creative briefs will give you: 1) a quick and succinct understanding of the research to date to ensure you keep the customer's needs top of mind and 2) direction and inspiration for where to focus your idea generation.

We'll use the creative briefs as springboards to generate ideas in the ideation workshop. In the meantime, please read and absorb them, allow your thoughts to incubate, note down any ideas and bring them along to the workshop.

I look forward to working with you in what promises to be a creative, collaborative and action-oriented workshop.

And then the set of creative briefs follows in the document.

3. DEVELOP YOUR CREATIVE STIMULUS

Do this in addition to your creative briefs. What creative exercises are you going to run? What people, tools, artefacts and space are you going to need for each exercise? Are you going to bring in any guest speakers for inspiration or go on any creative excursions?

4. DESIGN AND SET UP YOUR SPACE FOR THE SESSION

If possible book the venue for a couple of hours the day before, so you can set up everything in advance and do a dry run of the tech. It takes quite a while to prep all the flip charts/whiteboards and exercises, and it's nice not having to attend to all of that stuff early in the morning before everyone arrives.

5. FIND YOUR FACILITATOR

Find someone who is a great facilitator and can run the day. Too many project leaders facilitate their own workshops, but you can't be the referee and a player. It is best to delegate the facilitation and then you can participate in the ideation. If you do want to be the facilitator and develop your skills in this it is important you find your own style. This is one of the key things we teach in our 'train the trainer' and facilitation training courses. It's also the role of the facilitator to manage everyone's energy for the day.

WORKSHOP

Once you've set up the session then it all comes down to how you run the day and what you do. I've provided a skeleton for an ideation session. This is something that you can play around with and run anywhere from 30 minutes to several days (provided you have enough creative briefs and stimulating creative exercises to keep everyone going). Most ideation workshops I design and facilitate run between a half to two full days. Here is the skeleton flow:

» Set the Scene

» First Burst

» Idea Sprints

» Harvest

» Idea Canvas

» Showcase your Top Ideas

» Post-Workshop Debrief and Prioritisation

SET THE SCENE

It's really important that you make everyone feel welcome, included and important. This starts by having tea and coffee on arrival and food and refreshments at breaks. It also includes a heartwarming and inspiring welcome from the project leader or sponsor. This is also a good time to cover off any logistics and safety guidelines.

Then you want to give an overview of the program, what stage you are at and the objectives and timings for the day. The project leader and the facilitator should do this.

Next it is important to get everyone into the right frame of mind and exhibiting those creative behaviours I shared earlier—suspend judgement, understand the idea and build on the idea. This is also when I touch on any other house rules such as keeping mobile phones on silent and putting laptops away. A quick creative state exercise (energiser) and a reminder of the best behaviours for a brainstorm work well here.

Finally, I allocate people to their teams. This can be pre-planned to ensure a good split across functions and roles, or it can be done randomly using a sorting exercise. You can also make the sorting exercise into a bit of an icebreaker and a way for people to meet each other.

FIRST BURST

People often come in with some ideas already formed (and if you've circulated the creative briefs this is something you want). If it is an internal design project (such as to redesign onboarding) some people might even have ideas that they've been sitting on for years. It's important to give everyone time and space to get these off their chest first. This is critical because people are less likely to listen to and build on others' ideas until they've shared their long-harboured ideas first. I like to start with a 'first burst' for the overall challenge and not any specific creative briefs (you can find a home for the ideas that come from the first burst under the right creative brief if they get selected later). Either do this first burst in teams using the brainstorm rules and tips (suspend judgement, understand and build on each other's ideas), or give everyone 15 minutes to individually walk around the room and place ideas under each creative brief.

TIME	PEOPLE	MATERIALS
10 minutes	Core team of 4–8	A whiteboard or wall, flip chart paper, markers and sticky notes

1. **Set up.** Write 'First burst' at the top of a piece of flip chart paper or a whiteboard. Someone from each team volunteers to be facilitator, unless you have a designated facilitator for each group.

2. **Idea generation.** Individuals sketch and write their ideas, one per sticky note, and read them out to the group while passing them to the facilitator who puts them up on the flip chart. This physical handing over of the idea ensures it becomes the group's idea. Keep going until everyone has exhausted their ideas or time is up. Remember to build on each other's ideas as you go.

TIPS

» *Capture ideas.* Sticky notes work best and where possible I'd encourage people to include a sketch. Not only does this provide visual cues to the rest of the team, but it also warms up the creative side of the brain. Ideas should be written in the simplest possible way to make them easier to build and evaluate. Try simply writing them as: 'It is an X that does Y'. For example, Uber—it is a location based app that makes hiring an on-demand driver easy, convenient and safe.

» *Set a target.* I always set a target for each exercise, as it is motivating and teams will aim for it. You can also have a bit of fun rivalry between the teams and keep a tally going for the day. For first burst I tend to give them a target of 25 ideas in 10 minutes.

IDEA SPRINTS

Next we run parallel team idea sprints (a set of creative exercises) on each creative brief. Teams can comfortably brainstorm for three different creative briefs each in a day before they get a bit of mental fatigue. For each creative brief I cycle through four steps or exercises (mini brainstorms) to make up the idea sprint. The exercises I choose provide a good mix of individual thinking time and group brainstorming, so they cater to different personality and thinking types and increase the diversity of ideas. I also find you get the best results by starting with individual thinking time before progressing to group time. This allows everyone to jot down some initial ideas before having to share in a group. The idea sprint cycle is comprised of:

1. mind map

2. Crazy 8s

3. first burst (this is the first burst for this creative brief, so it's in addition to the overall first burst)

4. creative exercise.

1. MIND MAPS

Hopefully all the participants have read the creative briefs (if not then provide time now), incubated and thought of some ideas prior to the workshop. The first two steps in the idea sprint help flesh out any ideas from the incubation time, as well as firing everyone's brains up. Creating a mind map of all the thoughts and ideas they have for their first creative brief is a great way to start this. The mind map then becomes their stimulus for the next step. To set this up I simply give everyone a sheet or two of blank A4 paper, a marker pen and a time limit of five minutes.

1. Individually create a mind map of all your ideas for this creative brief—five minutes.

2. Quietly jot down all the ideas that are in your head, mix them with old ideas and new ones, and loosely map them on paper.

3. Write words, or draw pictures, and find connections. There is no right or wrong way. It's just what works for you. (See figure 4b.1, overleaf, for an example.)

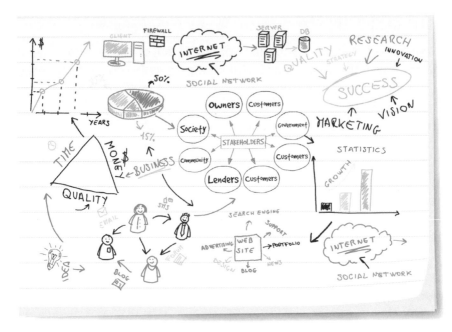

Figure 4b.1: example mind map

2. CRAZY 8S

I first learned this technique from a series of articles back in 2012 in *Fast Company*. Jake Knapp was writing about how he and his team run their five-day sprints in Google Ventures. I love this technique. Jake and some of his colleagues have since gone on to write a book on this and more of their techniques called *Sprint*. For our purposes I'll give you a quick overview of how we use the Crazy 8s.

1. *Sticky notes.* Jake and his team get each participant to fold a blank sheet of A4 paper in half three times, then unfold it, so you get eight panels. However, since we take the ideas from Crazy 8s straight into each team's first bursts, I get each person to use a pack of sticky notes.

2. *Five minutes.* Take five minutes total to sketch eight ideas, one per sticky note, 40 seconds per sketch.

Remind people that it isn't an art class, so there's no need to try and re-create the Sistine Chapel! They'll need to forget their self-judgement and just get their ideas down. Tell them if they get stuck, try creating a variation on an earlier sketch to keep things moving. Or as Jeremy Utley from d.school always says, 'If you're stuck having a good idea have a really crappy one first!' I just love that line.

The ideas everyone has come up with in this exercise will come into play in the next exercise.

3. FIRST BURST

Now the teams are back to running another group first burst, but this time on the first creative brief. The facilitator changes (unless you have a designated one in each group). Set a target of 25-plus ideas in 10 minutes, which, given you've already got multiple ideas from each person's Crazy 8s, you are going to blow this target out of the water. Everyone brings their Crazy 8 ideas and takes turns to share their ideas, with everyone else in the team riffing off them and building on them. Just remind everyone to keep using sticky notes and marker pens and build on each other's ideas, as they tend to fall back into old habits after one round.

Somewhere towards the end of the 10 minutes the teams will start to run out of ideas (see figure 4b.2). At this stage a pro facilitator would introduce a new creative exercise to look at the problem from a different angle and/or provide fresh stimuli. Or, if they've exhausted the creative brief, they'd switch to a new creative brief.

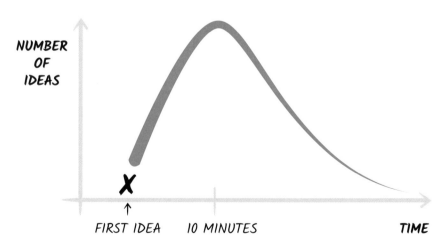

Figure 4b.2: diminishing ideas

Before moving on to a new creative brief I like to ensure we've exhausted the current one. And while it is hard work to keep squeezing ideas from the same creative brief, Jake Knapp says that sometimes the best ideas come when you are starting to 'scrape the bottom of the barrel'. So we move on to step 4 and introduce another creative exercise. Remember when I talked about the brain earlier in this chapter, and how it's linear and we have to use stimulus to trick it to think laterally? Well now that we've captured everyone's initial ideas we want to introduce lateral thinking to spark some fresh and more original thinking.

4. CREATIVE EXERCISE

Creative exercises are creative thinking techniques that get your brain thinking laterally, or outside of the box. One of my favourite creative exercises is Best in World—it's a classic lateral thinking exercise, so I like to start with it.

You can either bring the teams back into the plenary space or leave them standing in their groups to take them through a briefing and demonstration on this exercise. You would have already drawn up the exercise on flip chart paper or whiteboards in each team zone.

BEST IN WORLD

TIME	PEOPLE	MATERIALS
25–45 minutes	Groups of 4–8	A whiteboard or wall, flip chart paper, markers and sticky notes

1. *Setup.* Take two pieces of flip chart paper and create three columns. Write a heading above each column: Best in World, Principles and Ideas (see figure 4b.3).

2. *Best in World.* Take a few minutes and in the first column make a short list of organisations/brands/products/people, and so on, that face the type of challenge in this creative brief and solve it really well.

3. *Principles.* Then select a couple of the 'worlds' and write down all the principles for how they solved the challenge.

4. *Ideas.* Go through the principles and use them as inspiration to generate new ideas. Remember to build on each idea. Then go back to 'worlds' again and repeat the steps.

Figure 4b.3: Best in World setup

TIP

The key is moving from left to right. The rookie error most teams make is they get to the end of the allocated time and they've created big long lists of 'worlds' and 'principles', but haven't got to the ideas stage. Obviously, the first two are just the means to the ideas.

Table 4b.1 (overleaf) shows an example, which shows how roll-on deodorant was invented by borrowing inspiration from the ball point pen.

Table 4b.1: challenge: How might we apply deodorant more smoothly?

Best in World	Principles	Ideas
Who in the world solves this challenge of 'smoothly distributing liquids' really well?	How do they solve this challenge? What are the principles?	Borrow from the principles to solve your own challenge
Painters	Brushes	Roll-on liquid deodorant was invented
Paint roller	Dip in paint then roll onto the wall	
Knife	The knife spreads the substance	
Pens	Pen contains a ball that applies the liquid	

***

This completes your idea sprint for each team's first creative brief. At this stage you might take a short break of 15 minutes to refresh and refuel before moving onto each team's second creative brief and idea sprint, cycling through the four steps. I always keep steps 1 to 3 the same, but you can change up step 4 by switching in a different creative exercise. With practice you'll learn which creative exercises work best for which types of creative briefs. And it doesn't hurt to actually stress test the exercises on the creative briefs before the workshop. If you can't think of any ideas for the briefs using the exercise, then the participants probably won't be able to either. Once you've completed all of your idea sprints it is time to harvest the ideas and select the top ones to take forward.

CREATIVE EXERCISE GALLERY

Here are some more of our favourite creative exercises that you can play around with and try out in your workshops. Keep yourselves and your teams fresh by trying out a different one in each new workshop or project. All of them have been tried and tested by my teams many times over in many different countries, industries and challenges.

EXPERTS AS STIMULUS

TIME 60 minutes to 1 day	**PEOPLE** Pairs/ Group	**MATERIALS** Pen and paper

Talking to an 'expert' from another background can provide us with lots of fresh stimulus when coming up with new ideas.

1. Brainstorm a list of people who might give a fresh take on your challenge. For example, for making training more fun why not talk to a dog trainer or school teacher or fitness instructor?

2. Invite the 'expert' in to speak with your team, or go and meet them. Ask them to talk about their work and how they solve the 'challenge' in their work.

3. Identify how they have solved similar challenges and what the principles were.

4. Relate these principles back to your challenge to come up with new ideas.

DECONSTRUCTION

TIME 10–25 minutes	**PEOPLE** Groups of 4–8	**MATERIALS** A whiteboard or wall, flip chart paper, markers and sticky notes

A great creativity tool is 'deconstruction'. Simply deconstruct the challenge first and then reconstruct (create) solutions.

1. Make bullet point answers to the following prompts:
   - Describe the challenge. (For example, if it's an object: What is it made of? What shape is it? How is it made?)
   - Describe its function. (For example, Who uses it? How is it used? To what purpose?)

2. Generate new ideas for your challenge. Work your way through these individual elements (your answers to the two prompts above) and come up with new ideas for them.

BREAK THE RULES

 TIME
25–45
minutes

 PEOPLE
Groups of
4–8

 MATERIALS
A whiteboard or wall, flip chart
paper, markers and sticky notes

This is a great creativity tool. Breaking the rules consists of listing out all the rules or norms of the challenge and then challenging each one in turn. For example, Uber challenged the rules of a taxi service having to have its own fleet of cars and drivers by enlisting the public and their private cars as drivers. To break the rules:

1. *Setup.* Take two pieces of flip chart paper and create three columns. Write a heading above each column — Rules, Challenges and Ideas.

2. *Rules.* Take a few minutes and in the first column list all the rules/norms/status quo to your challenge.

3. *Challenges.* Take a few more minutes and write down challenges for each of the rules. Work your way through these individual rules.

4. *Ideas.* Go through the challenges and use them as inspiration to generate new ideas. Remember to build on each idea.

RANDOM CONNECTIONS

 TIME
25–45
minutes

 PEOPLE
Groups of
4–8

 MATERIALS
A whiteboard or wall, flip chart
paper, markers and sticky notes

Another great creativity tool is Random Connections. It's about selecting a random object or 'thing' to provoke us to think of novel ideas. For example, Swiss engineer George de Mestral was looking for a new way of fastening fabrics together. After a walk in the woods one day he wondered if the burrs that clung to his trousers—and dog—could be turned into something useful. The result was the invention of Velcro.

1. *Setup.* Take two pieces of flip chart paper and create three columns. Write a heading above each column—Random things; Attributes, values and benefits; and Ideas.

2. *Random things.* Select four to five random objects from around you and write them down in column one.

3. *Attributes, values and benefits.* Take a few minutes and list all the attributes, values and benefits for each random thing.

4. *Ideas.* Go through the attributes, values and benefits and connect to your challenge to generate new ideas. Remember to build on each idea.

HARVEST

You've done all this hard work over days (or most likely weeks) since the beginning of the project, and now you've got to select just a handful of ideas (for now) to take forward. How do you do it? I've always liked to use a mix of the heart and head (intuition plus logic) and in that order—first with the heart and then with the head. If we start with just the purely rational we often end up with incremental short-term ideas that are easily executable, but not very differentiated to what already exists in the market. By starting with our intuition we get to harness our inner entrepreneur first and choose the ideas that we'd run with if it was our own business, and then sense check the selection with our logic side. For example, my gut feel is telling me these ideas would be really desirable; now, using my head, do I think they meet the customer's needs and insight from the creative brief?

DESIRABILITY FIRST

Why desirability first? When I was working alongside Jeremy Utley and Perry Klebahn, Directors of Executive Education and Adjunct Professors at Stanford d.school, as part of New Zealand's Better by Design program for small to medium enterprises, we focused on starting with desirability and then prototyping and testing for feasibility and viability later in the innovation journey. This is because you've got all your creative, unique and fledgling ideas from your incubation and idea sprints. Then when you assess them with business-as-usual feasibility and viability criteria, you come up with the same old familiar and incremental solutions. This is partly because feasibility and viability are lenses of what we can currently do, so therefore they're more likely to favour more incremental ideas. Imagine if James Dyson had evaluated his ideas for the vacuum cleaner based on what was feasible and viable at the time? He would have said, 'Well, that isn't feasible' and we wouldn't have the Dyson vacuum cleaner. And he wouldn't have gone on to create the Dyson hand dryer, bladeless fan or hair dryer either! So it is really important that we don't restrict our innovative thinking too early in the journey by limiting our ideas to what is currently feasible and viable.

By selecting ideas for potential instead we can then prototype and test them for feasibility and viability later in the innovation journey. So we are holding off jumping into feasibility and viability for just a bit longer.

You can always run a second harvest to select ideas that you can feasibly and viably do now (core and incremental innovation) if that is one of your project objectives or business requirements.

So how do you select for desirability? Give everyone a means for individually voting (sticky dots work really well, but I've also used fake money or casino chips to add a bit of realness and tangibility). I recommend breaking the voting and selection down into four steps:

1. Issue everyone six dots/casino chips per creative brief. Enough so that you are going to get a heat map of the best ideas, once the voting is done, but not so many that every idea gets a vote. Remember you are going to have about 50-plus ideas per creative brief.

2. Ask everyone to individually read through all their team's ideas across all their creative briefs and make a note of which ideas they'll vote for (based on customer desirability), but don't put any stickers down yet, allowing around five minutes for reading per creative brief. We do it this way to avoid groupthink.

3. Give them five minutes to do the actual individual voting—placing the dots. This should be quick, as they've already decided where to vote. As mentioned, doing it in this order limits any groupthink.

4. Ask them to regroup as a team and select the top ideas from those with votes to take forward. And the haggling starts! There should be an agreed number of ideas per team, for example the top two per creative brief.

The right quantity to take forward comes back to time, money and resources to design, test and build them. I find two per creative brief works well, providing the right amount to take into the next stage and allowing for further harvesting in the subsequent steps. If you have four teams with three creative briefs each (12 creative briefs in total) then you'll have a total of 24 ideas to progress. I find they often harvest them down further through the Idea canvas step, which we'll do next.

If you want you can provide a bit more direction through some selection criteria around desirability, here are the selection criteria that we used with Jeremy Utley and Perry Klebahn on the Better by Design project. Each person gets six dots (two of each colour—red, yellow and green) per creative brief and:

1. with the red dots select the top two ideas per creative brief that are most likely to successfully address your customer insight

2. with the yellow dots select the top two ideas per creative brief that are most likely to delight customers

3. with the green dots select the top two ideas per creative brief that are most breakthrough/innovative/disruptive.

Putting this into practice you use the same steps as for voting with the dots, but give each team member two dots of each colour per creative brief (so if it's three creative briefs per team then six dots of each colour). Remember to get each person to individually read through and select their own ideas before voting to avoid groupthink.

TIP

If you're running more than two idea sprints it's a good idea to add the harvesting in at the end of each sprint. Otherwise, you end up with too many ideas to harvest in one go at the end of all the sprints. It becomes too big a volume of ideas for people's brains to digest, compute and assess. This does add a little bit of time, but is worth it. If you do adopt this approach be mindful that you are switching people in and out of creative and judging states, so clearly signal it each time and highlight the correct behaviours.

IDEA CANVAS

You've now got your short-listed ideas, somewhere around 24 depending on how many creative briefs and teams you have, but they're only really a handful of sticky notes with a few sketches and words. One of the worst mistakes to make is to stop there and come back to them in a day or two, after the team has dispersed, to write them up. You'll find that really tough to do. You'll wonder 'Why did we vote for that idea?!' Or, worse still, 'I don't even know what that idea is!'

So it is really important that you clearly capture and flesh out each of the top ideas and what they mean while they are fresh in your mind. Sticky notes alone aren't enough. What are needed are useful, actionable ideas—ideas that lead to innovation. This is where the idea canvas comes in. It provides:

» *a common framework*. The idea canvas provides a structured template for fleshing out your top ideas, making them all comparable, as well as aligning the team on what each idea actually stands for

» *rigour*. It helps you transition your fledgling ideas into rigorous ideas—adding some meat to the bones

» *a brief for the next phase*. The idea canvases serve as design briefs informing your concept and prototype development

» *a point of reference*. They also act as a point of reference you can refer back to during experimentation, updating your canvas to keep a record of the concept's evolution, checking you haven't lost the integrity of the original customer insight and idea, or, if elements have changed, documenting why.

The idea canvas (see figure 4b.4, overleaf) contains six key elements.

1. *The customer insight*. Who you are targeting and why. This directly transfers across from your creative briefs.

2. *The idea*. Your solution to the customer insight. This is where you flesh out what was on one of your winning sticky notes. Use the format described earlier in this chapter for capturing ideas—'it's an X that does Y'. It is also useful to start thinking about the idea further by listing its top three features. Below the idea and key features you can also capture any other key product or service details such as technical specifications, packaging or ingredients.

3. *Benefits and reasons to believe*. It is really important to articulate what the benefits to the customer are, remembering that the number one reason new startups and innovations fail is because there is no market for them—no-one wants them. It is also really useful to list the benefits to any partners and intermediaries and to your organisation itself. While we haven't tested our ideas for desirability yet it doesn't hurt to start articulating the value we believe it will create. Reason(s) to believe are the features and evidence that support the benefits, making them believable. For example, Dove won't dry your skin like normal soap, because it's one-quarter moisturising cream. Or Cadbury's chocolate is so creamy because it contains a glass and a half of milk per bar.

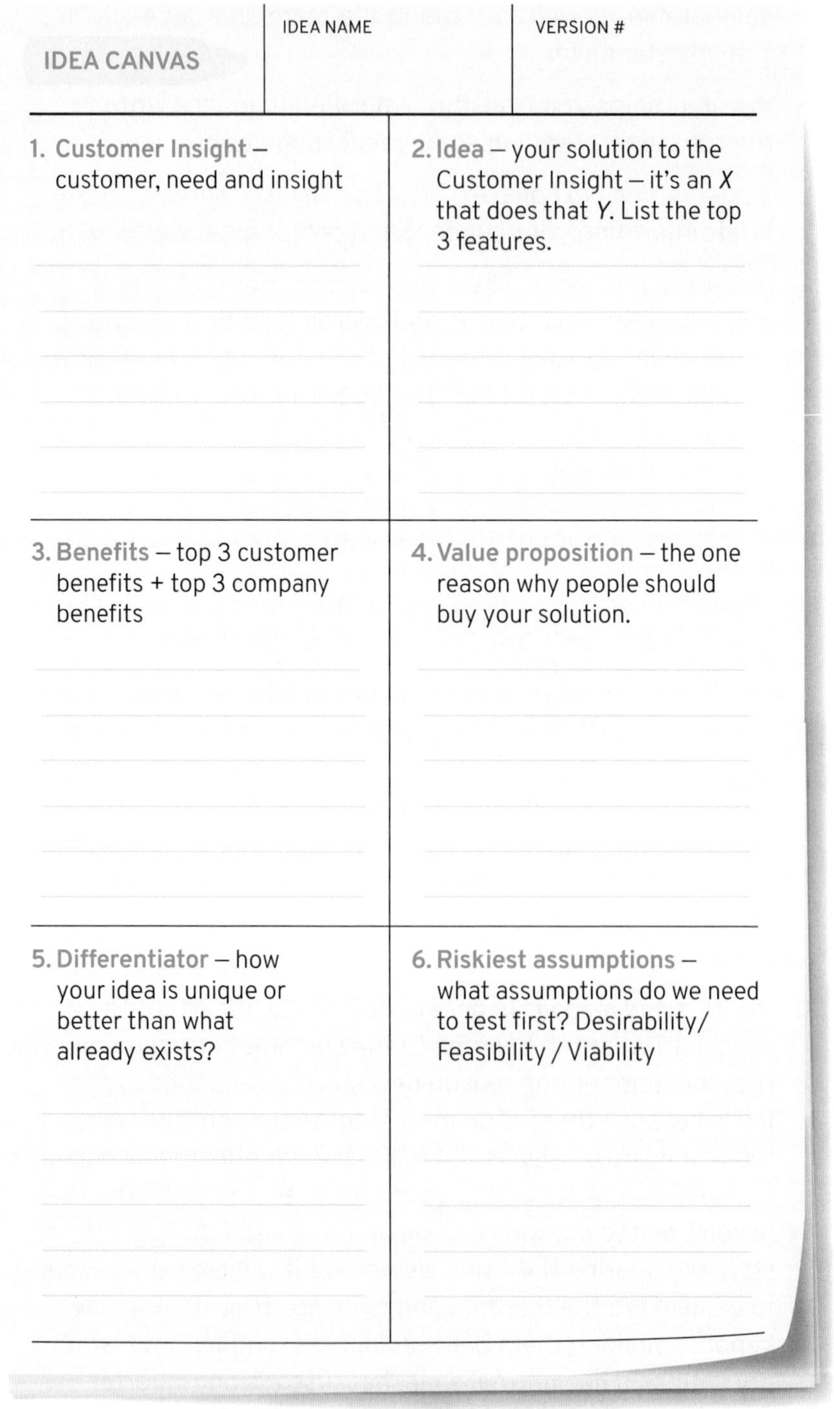

IDEA CANVAS	IDEA NAME	VERSION #

1. Customer Insight – customer, need and insight

2. Idea – your solution to the Customer Insight – it's an *X* that does that *Y*. List the top 3 features.

3. Benefits – top 3 customer benefits + top 3 company benefits

4. Value proposition – the one reason why people should buy your solution.

5. Differentiator – how your idea is unique or better than what already exists?

6. Riskiest assumptions – what assumptions do we need to test first? Desirability/ Feasibility / Viability

Figure 4b.4: idea canvas

4. *Value proposition.* This is the one reason why people will 'buy' your solution. It might be one of the benefits or a combination of them. Once again it is linked back to the customer insight.

5. *Differentiator.* How is this idea different from or better than what your organisation and competitors already do? If it isn't different or better, then there's no point doing it.

Often people get a bit confused between benefits, value proposition and differentiator. Just remember that benefits are the list of all the key benefits to the customer. The value proposition is that one key benefit or combination of benefits into a compelling statement as to why the customer should buy the product. And the differentiator is your discriminator or competitive advantage.

6. *Riskiest assumption(s).* The final box is for outlining what you perceive to be the riskiest assumptions—what hypotheses you have made. At this stage we focus on assumptions made about the desirability of the idea. Obviously, the key assumptions to test will be likeability and likelihood to purchase, but you may have other assumptions to test, for example we believe that the customer wants all the ingredients to be organic. Later on in the journey we'll move into feasibility and viability assumptions.

What I find works best for writing up the idea canvases is getting the people in each team to divide and conquer by divvying up the ideas among pairs. That way you get through the ideas quicker. You can then get other pairs from your team or even across the other teams to check and build on them.

EXAMPLE IDEA CANVAS

Here is an example idea canvas we post rationalised for an on-demand ride share company.

1. *The customer insight*
   - The key needs and pain points with taxis were around long wait times, not knowing how far away the taxi was, not being able to book taxis for a designated time (in some countries), slow payment on arrival at destination.

2. *The idea*
   - a location-based app that makes booking an on-demand private driver easy, convenient, inexpensive and safe
   - key features include: location-based app, tracking and easy payment

3. *Benefits*
   - on-demand availability
   - certainty—guaranteed ride
   - ETA—track the car while you wait
   - shorter wait time
   - cashless ride

4. *Reason(s) to believe*
   - location-based app and tracking
   - digital payment
   - driver and passenger experience ratings
   - drivers registered and screened

5. *Value proposition*
   - on-demand ride of your choice at your convenience

6. *Differentiators*
   - on-demand availability
   - certainty—guaranteed ride
   - ETA—track the car while you wait
   - shorter wait time
   - cashless ride

7. *Riskiest assumption(s)*
   - that people (passengers) would ride with strangers
   - that people (drivers) would want to drive 'randoms' in their private car

SHOWCASE YOUR TOP IDEAS

It's always good to finish any workshop on a high. To bring the workshop to a close get each team to showcase their idea canvases. This is a great opportunity to get everyone aligned and have other teams build on each other's ideas. You can either capture these on sticky notes as you go around the room or have someone type up all the comments as they happen. It is also a good time to bring in any key stakeholders and involve them in the showcase.

To round your ideas workshop off it is critical to thank everyone and talk the group through clear next steps and let them know how they can stay involved. For example, asking them to critique the concepts and prototypes before they go into testing. If you are going to be testing the concepts in focus groups with viewing facilities, they can come along and view the testing of their ideas with customers. Ask them for permission to follow up with them on any questions that come up when you are typing up the canvases. Even better, provide each team with a digital idea canvas template and deadline and ask them to type them up for you.

I always finish with everyone on their feet (more energy) thanking them again for their commitment, energy and ideas and tell them to give each other a big round of applause and then wrap it up.

POST-WORKSHOP DEBRIEF AND PRIORITISATION

I always find it useful to review the final idea canvases selected after a night's sleep and in the fresh light of day. What I find works best is to get the core team back together the next day for two to three hours. The objective for this session is to agree on which idea canvases to take forward into prototyping and testing. You'll have somewhere up to 24 idea canvases and probably want to get down to eight to 12 depending on how many different customer segments you'll be testing them with. As a guideline you don't want to be testing more than eight concepts in a two-hour focus test group.

Any more than this and you won't have time to test and explore them in enough detail. Given you'll want to test each concept more than once (more detail on this in the next chapter) then if you want to test more than eight concepts you'll need to run extra test groups. To help further refine the number of idea canvases down to eight to 12 we go through each one in detail and use a prioritisation framework to evaluate them for strategic fit and desirability. You can also add some viability criteria such as size of market to help prioritise based on the size of the prize, and for some quick wins add some feasibility criteria too. A mixed portfolio of ideas across time and innovation horizons is recommended to help manage short- to long-term organisational expectations and performance. See table 4b.2 for an example prioritisation framework with example criteria.

Table 4b.2: example prioritisation framework

		Idea 1	Idea 2	Idea 3	Idea 4	Idea 5
Strategy	Fit with business strategy	★★★★★	★★★★★	★★★★★	★★★★★	★★★★★
	Fit with innovation platform	★★★★	★★★	★★	★★★★	★★★★
Desirability	Meets an important customer need	★★★	★★★★	★★★★	★★★★★	★★★★
	Idea is unique or better than existing	★★	★★★	★★★★	★★★	★★★
Viability	Size of market	★	★★★★★	★★★	★★★★	★★
	Market growth/decline	★★★	★	★★★	★★	★★★★
Feasibility	Confidence to implement idea	★★★	★★★	★★	★★★★	★
	Portfolio type—incremental, evolutionarily, revolutionary	Incremental	Revolutionary	Incremental	Evolutionary	Evolutionary
Total		21	24	23	27	23

The Ideate stage is a big one, but it is also a lot of fun. You've turned your customer insights into creative briefs, incubated, planned and run workshops and generated stacks of ideas. You harvested them down and now you've got a short list of ideas fleshed out into rigorous idea canvases ready for briefing into design for prototyping and testing. We are getting closer to making your ideas real!

Learnings

- Great customer insights will naturally unleash creative thinking and fresh ideas.

- Incubation time is important and helps people absorb and immerse themselves in the customer need and insight statement and generate stronger ideas.

- You must intentionally get into an incubative and creative state to have good ideas. If you don't choose your state, your brain and body naturally choose it for you.

- People are more creative when they are able to be their full selves.

- Turn your customer insights into creative briefs to focus and inspire people's creativity.

- Our beliefs, behaviours, brains, state and environment can all block our creativity. We need to plan for and manage these in creative sessions.

- When harvesting your ideas don't jump to feasibility and viability too soon. This can result in all the new, different and breakthrough ideas being dropped before you have a chance to refine and validate them in experimentation.

- Make your ideas more robust by fleshing them out into the idea canvas.

Questions for innovators and leaders

- How do you currently encourage and promote creativity at your work?

- Is your culture supportive of asking questions and exploring ideas, or is the focus on there only being one right answer?

- Are people able to bring their full selves to work?

- In an era of busyness how do you allow your teams time for reflection, incubation and thinking?

- Do your people know when it's right to build on an idea and when it's the right time to judge?

- How do you and your teams get inspiration for new ideas and stay fresh?

- Are everyone's ideas treated equally regardless of seniority, expertise or role?

- Is your environment conducive and set up for both getting stuff done and being creative and experimental?

5A

EXPERIMENT

DESIRABILITY

In stage four, you and your team incubated and then generated ideas for your customer-centric creative briefs. You harvested them down and crafted the short-list into Idea Canvases. In stage 5a: Experiment, you'll develop these idea canvases into prototypes to test for customer desirability.

You've got a short list of creative ideas that you can be truly excited about, but since **stage 2: Discover** you've been working largely inside your lab in an 'abstract' world. Now it's time to get out into the real 'concrete' world and quickly and cheaply test if your target customers are equally excited about these ideas, and whether you have a feasible and viable business model.

Experimentation is a process of continually generating a broad range of hypotheses, prototyping and testing them in small-scale experiments, and feeding the more successful concepts while pruning the failed ones.

In this stage you'll prove the validity of your ideas by focusing on these four questions, adapted from startup expert Steve Blank:

1. Have we in fact identified a problem/need a customer wants to see solved?

2. Does our solution solve this customer need for a sizeable segment?

3. If so, do we have a viable and feasible business model?

4. Have we learned enough to go and build a business case to get funding for development?

Experimentation will help you successfully:

» prototype and test for desirability, feasibility and viability—the innovation sweet spot

» co-create experimentation briefs with partners across your innovation ecosystem

» use the Business Model Canvas to evolve your solution and identify, test and reduce the risk of your ideas

» build prototypes, run experiments, iterate and learn fast

» operate and make decisions in VUCA when there is insufficient data

» kill ideas that aren't desirable, feasible and viable, even if the stakeholder pushing for the idea is influential

» engage colleagues, partners and stakeholders with your ideas to create buy-in and momentum.

The first step in experimentation is to develop our idea canvases into prototypes, so we can test them for desirability with our hypothesised target customers.

PROTOTYPE

Prototyping is about bringing your ideas to life to make them testable in the quickest, cheapest and most low-fidelity way possible. As David Kelley, co-founder of IDEO puts it, 'Think with your hands, build something or try something, then talk about it, NOT the reverse'. This is where the term 'fail fast' comes from. At this stage it's not about whether you can make the product, service or experience, but rather whether, if it were made, it would matter to a group of customers.

Prototyping is also great for developing your ideas further (David Kelley calls it 'brainstorming with your hands'), and a great way of creating momentum and getting you moving when you are stuck.

I love the story about how Innocent Drinks in the UK did their prototyping. A few entrepreneurial young people who were getting tired of their corporate jobs noticed that people struggled to get their 'five a day' of fruit and vegetables. They thought 'What if we could make it easier for everyone by making 100 per cent natural fruit and vegetable smoothies?'

Rather than give up their day jobs without testing out their idea for desirability first, they made up some smoothies and set up a stall at a music festival in London to give out samples. A sign above the stall read 'Should we give up our day jobs to make these smoothies?' People were asked to throw their empties into bins marked 'Yes' or 'No'. They prototyped and tested the desirability of their idea first, before jumping into the more expensive development and commercialisation stages. If their idea had failed all they would have lost would have been a few days' work and the cost of a stall and some raw materials. But 'Yes' won, and the rest is history.

Prototyping is definitely one of the stages of innovation where customer-centric innovation and design has borrowed from traditional design and the design industry (graphic and brand designers, product designers and industrial designers). Many of the different types of prototyping now used come from this traditional design world. I'll explain a bit more about the following ways to prototype:

» concept boards

» storyboards

» roleplay

» physical prototypes.

CONCEPT BOARDS

The use of concept boards to articulate and test your ideas has been around a long time, especially in the fast-moving consumer goods (FMCG) industry. They're tried and proven and great for food and beverage innovation. This is how I first learned to design and test ideas in consumer research back in 2000 for Unilever. This was long before Design Thinking was big, and before design schools like Stanford's d.school even existed. With the advent of Design Thinking and Human-Centred Design people started to experiment, me and my colleagues included, with other ways to prototype our ideas, such as storyboards, making a product you can interact with and acting out roleplays for the customer to experience it. But I still find concept boards are a great initial prototype for many situations. For example, I've recently used them to test B2B digital platform concepts for one of Australia's largest fin-techs; data analytics service concepts for a leading university; importer and exporter concepts with a government department;

and B2B concepts in the mining industry, to name a few. They also help you articulate really well what your proposition is, forcing you to be single-minded.

A concept board is a tangible representation of your idea that makes it testable. In this case, it's in the form of a written concept with supporting visuals. The visuals might be a picture of the product or show key steps in the customer experience that you are redesigning.

These are the key elements of a concept:

» *Opportunity.* A powerful category and/or customer truth that exposes the opportunity—what problem are we solving, or what need are we satisfying?

» *Proposition.* A clear, focused and single-minded benefit(s). What potential solution does it represent?

» *Reason(s) to believe.* Your most relevant and compelling supporting evidence. What features/attributes can we draw on to help us make our case?

These three elements can be seen in figure 5a.1 (overleaf).

WRITING A CONCEPT

You can incorporate writing the concepts into your ideation workshops, following the creation of the idea canvases. Once again, I find this works best individually or in pairs. Alternatively, find a couple of people from the team who are really good at and enjoy copy writing and get them to do them after the workshops. You'll find it is quite an iterative process; it'll require a couple of rounds of editing and refining:

» Getting the opportunity 'balance' right is tricky—negative statements rarely work with customers. You can get inspiration here from your customer insight.

» Making the proposition single-minded and inspiring is key.

» You have to find the most compelling way to order and express benefits and the reason(s) to believe (selecting the real deal breakers).

Figure 5a.1: example On-Demand Ride concept board

TIPS

Here are some great concept-writing tips, many of which are inspired by fellow innovator and ex-colleague, Daniel Quinn:

» Your concept needs to connect with your audience.

» Make sure your concept is targeted to the customer. In order to do this, you have to know your audience—who exactly are you trying to connect with? Try sketching out a mini pen portrait/persona:

 - Who are they?

 - What do we know appeals to them?

 - If you were introduced to them at a party what would you speak to them about, and, more importantly, how would you talk to them?

 - What sort of language would you use to gain acceptance, and how would you get your point across?

 - How do other adverts that seem to have this audience in mind create connection?

» Make sure your concept strikes the right tone for your audience. Give it a distinctive and consistent style—something that feels real. Pay attention to:

 - the vocabulary you use

 - the length of your sentences

 - how you address the reader

 - whether the images strike the right tone for the audience.

» Make sure your concept is entertaining; if you bore people, they won't like your ideas. To get hold of and retain people's attention:

 - use superlatives judiciously

 - ban marketing speak; ask 'real' friends or partners to read them for a final check to be sure

- avoid words that the market has rendered dull or out of fashion
- use humour to give a warm, accessible feel to concepts
- use kick-ass visuals.

Once you've got a draft of your concept board, put it through the litmus test. Read what you've written out loud and ask yourself just one question: Does it sound cheesy?

If the answer is yes, then keep working at it. It's either now, or at the first research group.

STORYBOARD

Storyboards are great for visualising how a customer interacts with a process, service or experience. They're also a good substitute for when an idea is too difficult or conceptual to build into a tangible prototype. Storyboards are like a comic book that you and your team fill in, showing how the customer moves through the story—their movements, the information they input, their thoughts, and so on. See figure 5a.2 for an example of a storyboard.

To make a storyboard:

1. Create the panels—map out six to eight frames. You may not use them all, but that doesn't matter.

2. Fill in each individual step in the story with an image and a short description, showing how the customer progresses through the journey.

3. Stress test it on yourselves, then capture any learning and incorporate it.

4. Repeat steps 1 to 3 until you have built the minimum required to test with customers.

ON-DEMAND RIDE

Need a ride across town or exploring a city away from home?

Simply download the On-Demand Ride app and create an account.

Enter where you're going and be matched to a nearby driver.

Meet your driver. You can track their arrival on the map.

Sit back and enjoy the trip. When you arrive, payment is cashless and cardless.

Rate your trip. You can also give your driver a compliment or add a tip in the app.

Figure 5a.2: example On-Demand Ride storyboard

149

TIP

Make it stand-alone—you want your storyboard to make sense
by itself, without you there to demonstrate it. In testing you can
only be a guide at most.

ROLEPLAY

Another way to prototype and test an experience, process or service
is with a roleplay. The key to roleplays is to ensure an actual customer
does the testing. It's not about you and your team acting out being
the customer and falsely proving the idea works. (There is no harm
in practising and testing the roleplay without customers first, but at
some point you need to put it in front of real customers.) To develop
the roleplay:

1. Map it out—take each individual step in the experience and
   detail what happens in that phase. Identify the variable(s)
   you need to test to determine if it matters to the customer.
   Appoint roles for each step, and create physical prototypes
   that you'd like to test in the roleplay.

2. Practise the roleplay.

3. Capture your learnings—note down any learning and make
   iterations.

4. Repeat steps 1 to 3 until you have built the minimum required
   to test with customers.

PHYSICAL PROTOTYPES

A great way to understand whether your idea is as good in real life as
it is on paper is to build it.

1. Make it—use any readily available materials to bring it to life,
   whether it's foam board, plasticine, play dough, Lego or bits of
   scrap paper, plastic and string.

2. Stress test it on yourselves, then capture any learnings and make iterations.

3. Repeat steps 1 to 2 until you have built the minimum required to test with customers.

TIPS

» *Make it stand-alone.* Just like a real-life product, you should aim for your prototype to make sense on its own, without you there to demonstrate it. In the testing phase there will be a researcher to test the concepts, but the more it stands up on its own the easier it will be understood.

» *Identify a variable.* Build with the customer in mind—what do you hope to test with them? Identify the riskiest assumption (key hypothesis) that you want to test with each prototype and build that element.

» *Don't make it too polished.* Prototyping should be fun, fast, rough and ready. If it's too finished people won't comment on it.

» *Start doing.* Pick up some prototyping materials to get you going, even if you aren't sure what you're doing.

» *Keep moving.* Be sure to move quickly between prototypes to avoid getting too emotionally attached to it.

You and your team will be getting really excited now. There will probably be a lot of nervous energy. You've created your prototypes and you're now ready to start planning and running the testing phase.

TEST AND LEARN

It's time to find out whether your ideas are desirable. You've created your prototypes; now it's time to test.

'Test and learn' is an iterative process of researching and reviewing your prototypes with customers, getting feedback, making modifications and going through the loop again until you have a desirable concept (or not). If it is desirable then we progress to the next stage and run different experiments to test and develop it for feasibility and viability. If it's not desirable then we'll need to either pivot or perish:

» A *pivot* is a substantial change to one or more components of the concept, for example the target customer or value proposition. (Keep in mind that a minor change is an iteration, not a pivot.)

» *Perish* means to wind up (end) the project. You would wind up the project when the current concept isn't desirable and there is no perceived viable pivot available, or you are out of money or time.

Your first round of testing is not about finding whether you can feasibly build the idea. You want to find out whether, if you did build it, it would matter to the customer. The question is, 'Is it desirable?' In Lean Startup language this is known as 'problem-solution fit'. Remember, the number one reason innovations and startups fail is because they don't have a market — they're not desirable. If we prove it is desirable, then we can run experiments to develop the ideas for feasibility and viability.

Let's revisit the James Dyson example. He started by trying to solve a couple of important customer problems with vacuuming:

1. emptying the messy dusty bags

2. the vacuum cleaner losing suction power as the bag got full.

Now, if he'd assessed his ideas for feasibility and viability first he would have killed those ideas and we wouldn't have the Dyson vacuum cleaner we have today. Instead, once he had desirability he ran experiments to prototype, test and learn. Apparently there were over 5000 prototypes. So while desirability, feasibility and viability are equally important, it is about applying them at the right time to increase your chances of innovation success.

Early stage testing also provides another opportunity to explore your understanding of the customers and their needs. This empathy can lead to new insights and whole new ideas.

In the testing phase I always involve specialist researchers. These people live and breathe this type of work, doing it day in, day out. If you're strapped for cash then you can run the testing yourself, which is still better than not testing at all, but I'd highly recommend you find the budget to bring in the experts. In all the consultancies I've worked at we've always had either our own qualitative and quantitative researchers or freelancers to tap into. Working on the client side we've always had research managers who advise and manage this phase, bringing in the research agencies to run the testing. Either way I always engage specialist researchers with the right expertise to run this phase. People who don't do it at their own peril.

Testing for desirability is generally conducted through focus groups, or individual in-depth interviews in the case of some B2B concept testing, and both can be done either face to face or, in the case of remote location testing or scheduling challenges, through a number of emerging digital platforms such as online focus groups and discussions/bulletin boards. Here is some more detail on the most common approach, focus groups.

FOCUS GROUPS

How many focus groups should you run? Ideally, you run a new focus group for each customer segment until you stop getting any discrepancies in feedback from the customers (that is, you have corroboration of the feedback). If you need to budget for a set number of groups then I'd budget for a minimum of three groups per customer segment. If you only run one then you're at risk of it not being representative, and if you run two and there are large differences in feedback between the two then how do you know which group is more representative? By running a minimum of three at least you have a better chance of finding consistency.

For example, if we were testing our one-handed snack ideas on primary-school children we might want to split them by age brackets and gender to see if the responses are different. We might have three groups of girls aged five to eight and another three groups of girls aged nine to 12, and then the same for boys. If your budget was tight you could just do three groups of girls (two groups of one age bracket and one of the other age bracket) and three groups of boys, but if you find too many differences it will be hard to make a decision on which concepts to proceed with.

The duration of this phase depends on how many groups you're running. You need to allow two weeks to design the recruitment specification and discussion guide and recruit the customers. Your research manager or a researcher can help with this. There are also specialist companies called field recruiters that do the recruitment. This is important in avoiding any recruitment biases, such as recruiting friends and families and people from only one location. You'll need to provide the recruiters with a specification, which your research manager can help with.

When the groups are running, it is highly recommended that you and the team attend as many of the research groups as possible. Seeing is believing, providing you with a first-hand experience and context to review the recommendations and make a decision. It also gives you another opportunity to get more insight into your customers' world.

You will also need to allow one to two weeks for the researcher to analyse the results and write up the debrief following the groups. Don't rush this step, as, just like in stage 3: Distill insights, the gold is in the synthesis and insight generation. In total you are looking at four-plus weeks to plan, run and debrief your focus groups. (But the planning and recruiting can be run in parallel with the development of your prototypes.)

While you'll be keen to know the research results ASAP, the researcher cannot make any rigorous conclusions until all the research is completed and they have done their analysis. You should do the same — stay open until the debrief presentation.

DEBRIEF

The debrief is a good opportunity to get the core team and key stakeholders along for buy-in, commitment and understanding. At or following the debrief, your team and management need to decide the next steps. Desirable concepts can be progressed to the next stage of experimentation to be prototyped and tested for feasibility and viability. The remaining concepts will either need to be refined and retested, or pivoted or perished.

5 B

EXPERIMENT

In stage 5a you developed idea canvases into prototypes and tested them for customer desirability. In stage 5b, you'll take the desirable concepts into business modelling to run further experiments for feasibility and viability. The concepts that pass this stress testing for desirability, feasibility and viability are then prioritised for development and commercialisation. Those that didn't make it are pivoted or perished.

We've tested our concepts and identified which ones are to be perished or pivoted and which are the desirable ones that we can progress. Finally, we can jump to expensive and time-consuming business cases, right? Well, wouldn't you want to use the same Design Thinking methodology to quickly and cheaply prototype and test your concepts for feasibility and viability too? Well, that's what this next step is about. Helping you identify if:

» there is a sizable market for your solution

» you have a feasible and viable business model

» you have learned enough to go and build such a business case.

And with the advent of Alexander Osterwalder's Business Model Canvas and the Lean Startup methodology developed and refined by Steve Blank, Eric Ries and Ash Maurya, to name a few, we now have some great tools for developing, testing and de-risking the feasibility and viability of our ideas at a concept level before we go and invest large amounts of time and money into business cases and actual development.

I've seen many organisations and individuals start their innovation journey with the Business Model Canvas: they have an idea and immediately start to fill out the canvas. In my view, based on experience, there is no point completing a Business Model Canvas for an idea if you don't yet know it's desirable. This is just waste. We need to start with a problem that we know customers want to see solved, develop an idea that solves this problem, test this, and *then* use the Business Model Canvas to build a feasible and viable business model. This is illustrated in figure 5b.1, which shows how I've been using Design Thinking, Business Model Canvas and Lean Startup to innovate better, cheaper and faster. Following Design Thinking and the prototyping and testing of solutions to see if they are desirable, we add the Business Model Canvas to map out the feasibility and viability elements of your solution. We then iterate between the Business Model Canvas and Lean Startup–style experiments to de-risk and validate the solution and business model.

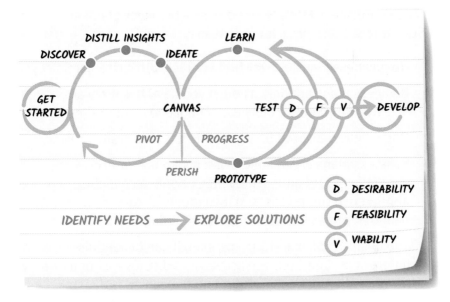

Figure 5b.1: integrated design-led innovation

BUSINESS MODEL THINKING

Business models are important. As Open Innovation expert Henry Chesbrough said, 'A mediocre technology pursued with a great business model may be more valuable than a great technology exploited via a mediocre business model'.

Why develop a business model? Because, as startup expert Steve Blank says, 'your idea isn't a business' and the Business Model Canvas helps you look at your idea (solution) at the business model level while also including all the inherent risks that still remain in your concept. As Blank has said, 'Every business model has a degree of uncertainty. Whether it is a new product, market or technology, each adds risk'. So before we go and build a business case or write our business plan we need to prove our business model. We do this by identifying our riskiest assumptions, turning these into hypotheses and then designing and running experiments (prototype-test-learn) to validate them. Remember, if you are innovating you are coming up with something new for the future. No data exists for the future, so the experimentation method is key.

Why use a Business Model Canvas over a business plan? According to Steve Blank there are a lot of reasons:

» No business plan survives first contact with customers.

» Business plans are only useful if you have to satisfy an investor who went to business school and wants to see one.

» Once it has delivered financing it is fundamentally useless.

» Business plans are mistaken as a cookbook for execution; people fail to recognise that they're only a collection of unproven assumptions, and it suddenly becomes an operating plan that drives hiring, firing and spending.

» The business plan is static, meaning it can't change as different assumptions are proven and disproven; but in reality no innovation project is static, and the canvas is dynamic.

THE BUSINESS MODEL CANVAS

The Business Model Canvas is covered in more depth in the fabulous book *Business Model Generation* by Alexander Osterwalder and Yves Pigneur. But for now here is a summary from the book to equip you with the knowledge to use it on your innovation journey.

The Business Model Canvas (see figure 5b.2) consists of nine basic building blocks that describe how a concept intends to create, deliver and capture value for the organisation and its customers.

The nine blocks cover off the four main areas of developing a new business or innovation:

1. customers
2. offer
3. infrastructure
4. financial viability.

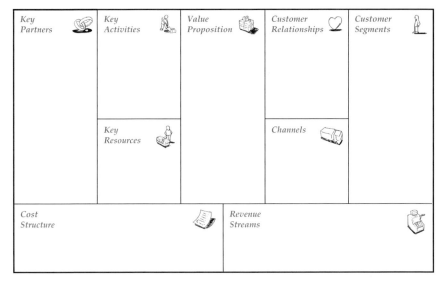

Figure 5b.2: the Business Model Canvas

Source: Alexander Osterwalder and Yves Pigneur, *Business Model Generation* (Hoboken, New Jersey: John Wiley & Sons, 2010)

BUSINESS MODEL CANVAS VERSUS LEAN CANVAS

There are a few modifications or alternatives to the Business Model Canvas, with one of the most popular being the Lean Canvas by Ash Maurya (see figure 5b.3, overleaf). I actually really like the Lean Canvas and find my thinking aligns a lot with Ash's. I like how the Lean Canvas articulates the problem and not just the customer segment, and similarly articulates the solution and not just the value proposition. And the Lean Canvas's unfair advantage is a lot like my differentiator in the idea canvas (used in stage 4). Have we copied the Lean Canvas in generating our idea canvas? No, these are all elements that I've used and evolved in innovation projects for the last 19 years, but it is great to see validation and like-minded thinking from another expert in this space.

For this stage of the innovation journey, though, I prefer the Business Model Canvas (with some modifications) because, as its name suggests, it looks at the whole business model, not just the product. Remember, we already have the idea canvas from stage 4: Ideate, which looks at the product or service really well. Also, the competitive advantage for your concept may come through another element of the business model than the product; just think how Uber and Airbnb have disrupted the market through new business models.

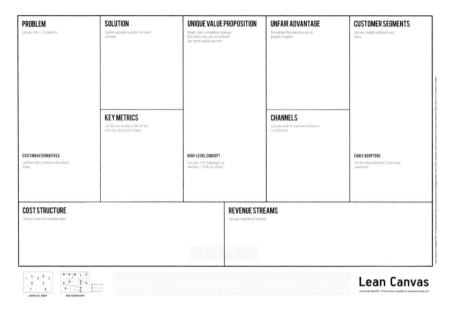

Figure 5b.3: Lean Canvas

Is the Business Model Canvas perfect? Maybe not, but I think what Osterwalder has created is fantastic and, much like Ash Maurya, I offer a few suggestions for improving how you can use it based on my experience using it both on real innovation projects and in training teams in innovation.

MODIFIED BUSINESS MODEL CANVAS

Here is how I like to use the Business Model Canvas for innovation (see figure 5b.4). First of all, it should flow and build on from the idea canvas that was created in the previous stage. Secondly, it should start with the customer and not the value proposition. You'll see the key elements of the idea canvas in stages 1 and 2. These are the key differences and you'll also notice that they correlate strongly with some of the key differences created in the Lean Canvas.

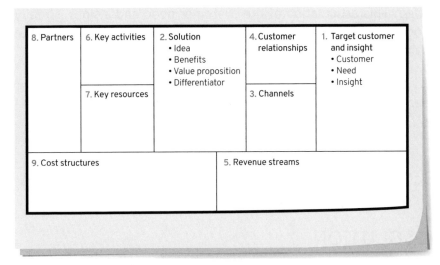

Figure 5b.4: modified Business Model Canvas

Source: Adapted from Alexander Osterwalder and Yves Pigneur, *Business Model Generation* (Hoboken, New Jersey: John Wiley & Sons, 2010)

1. TARGET CUSTOMER AND INSIGHT

The first modification I've made to the Business Model Canvas is to start with the customer and not the value proposition. As you would have already guessed from this book, I'm not a big fan of jumping to the solution. So I like to start with who the customer is and what problems I'm solving for them, which are articulated by the customer insight statement discussed in **stage 3: Distill insights.**

It is really important to be targeted with who your customer is and not try to be all things to all people. I've seen the customer be described too simply and broadly in people's use of the Business Model Canvas, for example describing the Nespresso customer as 'all households'. This is way too broad; even if we said 'all households who drink coffee' this would still be too broad and inaccurate. The target customer for Nespresso is a lot tighter than that and would include characteristics such as 'coffee lover' and 'aficionado'. The Business Model Canvas also doesn't call out the customer problem (needs and insight) we are solving. For example, for the Nespresso example the need(s) would be around 'wanting a café-style coffee but don't have the time to go out for one', or 'is willing to sacrifice some quality to save time, but wants something better than instant coffee'. This articulation of the customer need and insight is really important and shapes the value proposition and the rest of the business model, so I add this in.

In this section of the canvas we carry across and refine our customer need and insight from the idea canvas. For example:

- » *Target customer is:* indulgent foodies
- » *Needs and insights:* **need** guaranteed satisfaction, **because** if the delivered pleasure falls short of the expectation it doesn't justify the guilt.

2. SOLUTION

This is the other main element that I've modified in the Business Model Canvas. Not only is it really important to have a clear and single-minded value proposition, it is really important to carry forward the key elements from the Idea Canvas. This includes a detailed summary of the idea, including:

- » *The idea.* Your solution to the customer insight plus the top three features.
- » *Benefits.* Key customer benefits, plus the key benefits to any intermediaries and your organisation.
- » *Value proposition.* How this solves or satisfies a customer need or problem. This is the one single reason why people will 'buy' your solution. It might be one of the benefits or a combination of them. It is linked back to the customer insight.
- » *Differentiator.* How is this idea different from or better than what your organisation and competitors already do?

3. CHANNELS

Channels are how your solution is communicated and delivered to your target customer. Channels can be physical, for example, supermarkets, and/or web and mobile, for example, an app. Once again take a customer-centric approach and seek to understand what channels your customers prefer and work best for them.

4. CUSTOMER RELATIONSHIPS

This is where you capture how you *get, keep and grow* your customers; define the type of relationship you are trying to build with your customers; and define the type of relationship they would like with your organisation.

5. REVENUE STREAMS

This is where you capture how your idea is going to make money (or capture value) from each target customer. What value is the customer paying for and at what price? How are you going to monetise your idea?

6. KEY ACTIVITIES

Here you identify the most important activities that your organisation must do to make the idea work and deliver the right-hand side of the canvas (solution, channels and customer relationships). Think about the key activities that would be required of the front, middle and back of office.

7. KEY RESOURCES

Key resources are the most important assets that your organisation needs in order to perform the key activities and deliver the right-hand side of the canvas (solution, channels and customer relationships). Once again think about the key resources for the front, middle and back of office.

8. KEY PARTNERSHIPS

What are the key activities that you shouldn't be doing and perhaps don't want to do? Who are the key partners and suppliers needed to do these activities and make the innovation work? What key resources are you acquiring from them? What key activities do they perform?

9. COST STRUCTURE

What are the important costs of operating the new innovation? Consider your fixed and variable costs, and how you might achieve economies of scale.

***

Osterwalder and Pigneur talk about the right-hand side of the canvas (target customer and insight, solutions, channels, customer relationships and revenue streams) being your value creation and the left-hand side (key activities, key resources, key partners and cost structure) being your cost implications (see figure 5b.5).

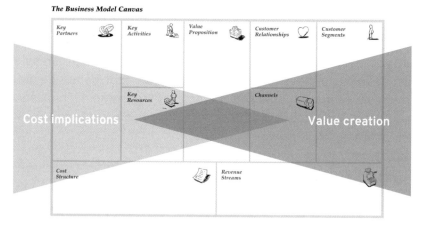

Figure 5b.5: cost implications and value creation

Source: Alexander Osterwalder and Yves Pigneur, *Business Model Generation* (Hoboken, New Jersey: John Wiley & Sons, 2010)

When I was working with fellow innovation and design consultant Matt Anderson he suggested a way to further articulate the link and flow from Design Thinking into Business Model Thinking. The idea is to overlay the DVF model—desirability, feasibility and viability with the Business Model Canvas—to show which elements of the Business Model Canvas relate to desirability, feasibility and viability. In addition to each relating directly to the value proposition, this means:

» Desirability relates to customer segments, value proposition, channels and customer relationships.

» Feasibility relates to key activities, key resources and key partners.

» Viability relates to cost structure and revenue streams.

BUSINESS MODEL DESIGN

TIME 45 minutes	**PEOPLE** Groups of 4–8	**MATERIALS** A whiteboard/flip chart paper, markers and sticky notes

STEP 1: CREATE A BUSINESS MODEL CANVAS

Draw up our modified Business Model Canvas using a whiteboard or flip chart paper (I recommend two sheets). Use your Idea Canvas as your start point. (It won't have all the answers; you'll have to make some informed guesses.) Follow steps 1 to 9 of the Modified Business Model Canvas in the recommended sequencing (starting on page 164). Use sticky notes to fill out the canvas (assigning a different colour of sticky note for each target customer group).

> ## TIP
>
> The canvas is a set of assumptions or guesses. It's okay to make guesses because we are in experimentation mode; we'll change the guesses into facts through testing.

STEP 2: IDENTIFY RISKS

Every business model has a degree of uncertainty. Whether it's a new product, new market or the use of new technology, each adds risk, as Steve Blank has observed. The focus of this stage is to efficiently identify which of our assumptions pose the greatest risk, so we can then systematically de-risk the business model through experiments.

Once we identify the risky assumptions, we turn them into hypotheses that can be tested. For example:

» *Assumption:* An idea or statement that something is true, without proof to back it up. For example, people will happily travel with private car drivers for transportation.

» *Hypothesis:* An assumption stated in such a way that it can be tested as true or false. For example, we believe that the public will happily travel with private car drivers for paid transportation.

169

To help identify the riskiest assumptions, I use a simple framework I call the Risk Matrix (see figure 5b.6), which I developed with Matt Anderson and is an adaptation of other matrices like the PICK matrix, which is a Lean Six Sigma tool, developed by Lockheed Martin. The Risk Matrix captures the critical assumptions in your business model, which are both uncertain and important for the success of the innovation endeavour. If you've seen another organisation or industry do what you're thinking of doing, then it's less risky. For example, when exploring the idea that would become the iPod Apple could have looked to Sony Walkman as to whether people are comfortable playing music to themselves in public.

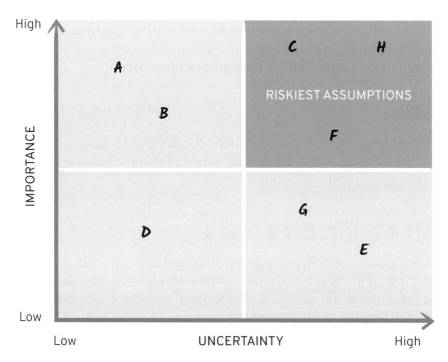

Figure 5b.6: Risk Matrix

Assumptions	Hypotheses
H	We believe that the public will feel safe travelling with private drivers.
C	We believe that the public will happily pay private car drivers for transportation.
F	We believe that private drivers will happily drive the public (strangers) in their cars for payment.

TIME	PEOPLE	MATERIALS
25 minutes	Groups of 4–8	A whiteboard/flip chart paper, markers and sticky notes

1. Draw up a Risk Matrix on a whiteboard or flip chart.

2. Review the canvas and highlight sticky notes that are guesses (assumptions).

3. Map the key assumptions underlying your business model on the Risk Matrix, plotting them based on the degree of importance the assumption has in the success of your business model and the degree of uncertainty you have about the assumption.

4. Identify your riskiest assumptions (top right box) that need to be tested as quickly as possible.

5. Write your riskiest assumptions up as hypotheses that can be tested as true or false.

STEP 3: DESIGN EXPERIMENTS

Now we can start designing experiments to prove or disprove our hypotheses, de-risking our business model and validating the feasibility and viability of our concept. First we create an experiment brief, which will help us plan experiments for testing our stated hypotheses.

1. Take the riskiest hypothesis.

2. Identify what you want to learn.

3. Design the test, identify target customers — who and how many, success criteria, duration of testing and action you will take if it passes or fails.

4. Define what stimulus (for example, discussion guide and/or prototype) you need for this test.

Remember, the focus is on testing to learn, so be clear on what you want to learn. The trick is to identify the most efficient way to test the riskiest assumption and gain validated learning. Figure 5b.7 (overleaf) is an example of an experiment brief.

IDEA NAME	On-Demand Ride
EXPERIMENT NUMBER AND DATE	#3 — 1 March 2008
HYPOTHESIS	We believe that private drivers will happily drive the public (strangers) in their cars in return for payment.
TARGET LEARNING	To understand if there is a supply side to our solution
TEST TYPE	Quantitative survey
SEGMENT	Suppliers
SUCCESS CRITERIA	5% of those tested will say yes
DURATION	4 weeks to set up, run and analyse the test
ACTION	Validated: move to next riskiest assumption
	Invalidated: pivot to different supply model
STIMULUS/ PROTOTYPE	Survey

Figure 5b.7: experiment brief

STEP 4: PROTOTYPE AND TEST

The next steps are to build the stimulus (for example, discussion guide, prototype) required to test your hypothesis and run the test as expediently as possible. Just like when you tested desirability, you may choose to use specialist researchers to run the test and designers to build your prototypes.

If you're running the test yourself, here are some guidelines:

» Let the customers experience the prototype and react to it rather than watch you do a presentation or demonstration, which won't give you the same insights. Remember: you are testing, not pitching! Listen more than you talk, actively observe them and don't correct misuse. Rather, learn from their improvisations.

» Have them talk through their experience and follow up with questions. Answer their questions with questions, for example if they ask, 'Would it include X?' reply by saying, 'What would you like it to include?'

» Be aware of the subtle difference between customers' feedback that they 'like' your concept and the actual likelihood they'll use it. I've been in many tests where the customers say they like it and we all get excited, only for the research moderator to then ask, 'And would you buy it?' and the customer replies, 'Ah, no thanks'. As you progress through your experimentation journey you need to rigorously test this commitment or willingness to pay. We do this by getting the customer to perform a call to action. (For example, getting customers to click on a 'plans and pricing' button on a landing page, or pre-purchase via a crowd-sourcing platform, or purchase your minimum viable product.)

» Analyse the results to capture learning and ensure they validate or invalidate your hypothesis.

» See 'Experiment gallery', starting overleaf, for examples of the types of experiments you can undertake.

TIPS

» Where it makes practical sense, test in the context in which the customer would actually use your solution.

» Design team roles, for example a moderator who transitions the customer from reality to prototype situation and guides (not leads) the testing. You may wish to enlist professional researchers. If you are roleplaying an experience you may need actors. Remember that team members and actors shouldn't play the customer role; this should be saved for the real-life customers. And have some team members to observe and take notes for analysis after the test capturing likes, dislikes and ways to improve, new questions to explore and new hypotheses and ideas.

» Remember you are not just validating your hypotheses, but trying to uncover why? Use the skills and tips you learned in **stage 2: Discover**.

» Remember this mantra: 'Prototype like you're right; listen like you're wrong'.

» You may find your experiment did not quite go according to plan. This is where you redesign the experiment.

EXPERIMENT GALLERY

There is no definitive rulebook on when to use which experiments. However, this should be directed by what you want to learn—what assumption you are testing. In the beginning uncertainty for your solution is high, so as a guide experiments should be low-fidelity and low-cost, keeping the cost of failure low. A prototype doesn't usually have to be very complex in order to learn what you need to know. In fact, you'll be surprised at how much quality feedback a customer can give you on a storyboard sketch that is far from perfect. Importantly, you'll learn much faster than if you had waited to build something more polished. As you progress through the journey and certainty increases you can spend more on higher fidelity experiments, remembering the primary goal is testing the riskiest assumption in the most efficient manner. Here I will go into the following types of experiments:

» landing pages and smoke tests

» demonstration and explanation videos

» concierge MVP

» Wizard of Oz MVP

» lo-fi wireframing

» hi-fi prototype

» market sizing and costs.

LANDING PAGES AND SMOKE TESTS

A good 'call to action' experiment for testing the demand of a product or service from real customers which requires minimal investment (no coding, no product required, little time and little money) is a landing page. It works by building a simple webpage to validate a specific assumption of your business model, such as the customer segment, value proposition or pricing. You then drive some traffic to the webpage (for example, through a tweet), which is one call to action, and upon landing offer further calls to action for the visitor to act on, for example to click on a 'plans and pricing' button.

You then measure the success of the experiment by analysing data collected from the landing page and through follow-up emails and/or phone calls to visitors to maximise the learnings from the experiment.

Example: Buffer's landing page

Buffer is an app that allows you to schedule your social media posts and tweets so you can build a consistent social media presence.

This idea arose from a personal pain point of Buffer's founder, Joel Gascoigne, in needing to manually plan and spread out his tweets throughout the day. Rather than jumping straight to building the solution like he'd done on his previous startup, without much success, he wanted to first test whether other people had this pain and whether they would consider using the app.

He created a simple landing page that described the value proposition – what Buffer would do for you. He then tweeted out a link to the landing page. On the landing page there was a call to action to click on 'plans and pricing' if you were interested. This took you to a second page, which said: "Hello. You've caught us before we're ready." And asked 'if you'd like an update on when we're ready' to enter your email. For visitors who left an email address he was able to follow-up with them personally and ask why they were interested. This validated that the pain did exist for others and there was some demand for the app. However, he wasn't ready to start building yet. He still needed to understand what people were willing to pay for it?

He then simply added a page in between the two, which showed three pricing plans: Free, $5 per month, $20 per month. The extra step tested the pricing by detecting which plan they clicked on and also tested further the demand for the product by adding an extra click.

Gascoigne said of the experiment, 'The result of this experiment was that people were still clicking through and giving me their email and a small number of people were clicking on paid plans. After this result, I didn't hesitate to start building the first minimal version of the real, functioning product.'

In this experiment, the landing page and Gascoigne's interactions with visitors served to validate the concept. Visit buffer.com to read more about this startup story.

DEMONSTRATION AND EXPLANATION VIDEOS

A good experiment for explaining complex concepts and business models is a demonstration video. These are simple and short video presentations used to showcase how the product is meant to work and the benefits to the customer. They drive a higher level of understanding and engagement through visual storytelling and are also sharable, which can help start building early awareness and even demand.

You measure success by analysing responses and data collected from the demo page (for example, using Google Analytics or kissmetrics) to track expressions of interest and attract signups.

Example: Dropbox demo video

The Dropbox demo video story is covered in more depth in the fabulous book *The Lean Startup: How Today's Entrepreneurs Use Continuous Innovation to Create Radically Successful Businesses* by Eric Ries. But for now, here is a short version to show how this type of experiment works.

Dropbox is a very easy to use file-sharing tool that today has over 100 million customers. However, it wasn't always that way.

The problem that Drew Houston and his team were trying to solve was file synchronization, but this was a latent need that most people didn't realise they had. The Dropbox team hoped that once people experienced the solution, they wouldn't be able to imagine life without it.

Their challenge was to explain this very technical and complicated concept, but as this couldn't be done through a standard product prototype, they instead created a video.

The video, narrated by Houston, offered a simple three-minute demonstration of how the solution works. While he explains, the viewer is watching his computer screen and seeing his mouse drag and drop files. Based on the customer reactions and qualitative feedback received, Drew validated his riskiest assumption.

CONCIERGE MVP

Another great 'call to action' experiment is the Concierge MVP, where you manually guide (and serve) your customer through a curated version of your intended solution to their problem. This experiment is also a great way for iterating and co-designing the solution with the customer, as it is very high touch with regular interactions.

Success is measured by interviewing the customer during and after the experience to gauge whether the solution satisfies their needs. It also allows for improvements to be identified, to establish what is needed to acquire or retain the customer, and to gauge what and if they will be willing to pay for it.

Example: Food on the Table

Food on the Table, a startup founded by Manuel Rosso and his VP of product, Steve Sanderson, is designed to help families eat better and save money at the grocery store.

But before they began coding, Rosso and Sanderson visited their local supermarket in Austin, interviewing shoppers to find any who were interested in the service. They then returned weekly to visit them, bringing a shopping list and selected recipes chosen based on:

» the customer's preferences

» promotions in the local store.

The list was updated frequently based on the customer's desires and feedback. Most importantly, Manuel and Steve would receive payment for this service.

With each weekly visit, they learned more about what their customers wanted, adding customers until they couldn't take any more.

Then they started coding.

WIZARD OF OZ MVP

The Wizard of Oz MVP is like an amalgamation of the Landing Page and Concierge MVP experiments. It works by putting up a front that looks like a real working product, but with you manually carrying out product functions behind the scenes. It's also aptly known as 'Flinstoning'.

Once again, it is a low-cost experiment that can help you move very quickly as you don't need to solve many technical fulfillment issues. It also allows you to test a 'call to action' and start charging for the service, making it great for testing and validating:

» problem-solution fit.

» your value proposition.

» market demand for your product or service.

» pricing.

Success is measured by reviewing the conversion rate, acquisition numbers and other metrics in a set period of time. You should also conduct follow-up emails and/or phone calls to the customers to maximise the learning.

Example: Zappos

A great example of a Wizard of Oz experiment is how Nick Swinmurn started Zappos. Swinmurn had the inspiration for an online shoe retailer when he failed to find a pair of brown Airwalks at his local mall. He wanted to test if other people had similar frustrations and whether his solution would solve the problem for a sizeable market.

Rather than jumping to building an expensive website, renting warehouse space and developing a full supply chain, Swinmurn went to his local shoe store and asked if he could take photos of their shoes and list them on his website. If he sold them, he promised he'd come back to the store and pay full retail price.

Through this experiment Swinmurn was able to learn whether there was problem–solution fit and market demand for his proposition. It also taught him key principles of how to run an online shoe retail business such as how to take payments, answer customer questions and accept returns, all without doing the time-consuming and expensive setting up of a full-scale operation.

Obviously, similar to Food on the Table's Concierge MVP experiment, Zappos' Wizard of Oz experiment wasn't scalable in its current format, but it validated many of his riskiest assumptions quickly and cheaply.

LO-FI WIREFRAMING

A lo-fi Wireframe is great for when you are making design and content choices and you want to get customer or product owner feedback.

A wireframe is the basic representation of a structure or customer interface without the graphical design treatment. It shows the main content (what), the structure of information (where) and a description of the customer interaction (how).

It is valuable because you can:

» show key elements of the final product for a low cost

» develop wireframe easily and quickly

» clearly visualize the product

» quickly evaluate multiple design concepts.

Success is measured through in-depth interviews or focus groups with customers and key stakeholders.

HI-FI PROTOTYPE

A hi-fi prototype is good for testing final designs, usability and functionality, as it is more realistic and closer to the final product. However, as it is more costly and time intensive to build and iterate than lo-fi prototypes, its use is normally reserved until the solution is relatively certain. This type of prototype is a high-tech and high-fidelity design of the concept, with partial to complete functionality, but linkage between the interface and back-end mechanisms is often omitted to reduce costs and speed up development cycles.

Success is measured using analytics to test metrics such as conversion, speed and stability and through continuous customer testing and follow-up interviews, including observation.

MARKET SIZING AND COSTS

While this isn't a replacement for full business case financials, like the other elements in the Business Model Canvas we need to validate the numbers behind our proposition. You can work out the estimated market size using the following approach.

» *Total Available Market.* This is a good place to start. Identify the size of the Total Available Market (TAM) by asking: of the total population how many people could want/need your product? For example, let's say we were developing a portable breakfast product for the Australian adult market. We do a Google search and find there are ~19 million adults in Australia and ~85 per cent regularly eat breakfast. TAM = 16.15 million.

» *Segmented Available Market.* The SAM is the portion of the TAM that you will target. The size of the SAM could be identified through a survey. For example, we identify that one in five adults who regularly eat breakfast express a current need for portable breakfast. So the SAM is 3.23 million.

» *Share of Market.* The SOM is the share of SAM that you believe you will get. What penetration? For example, because we are an existing cereal manufacturer with strong distribution channels we believe we'll get a 25 per cent SOM (807 500 people) in year one. From this we could even calculate our revenue. For example, from our research we know that our SAM would eat a portable breakfast three days per week and would pay $9 for a three-pack. Year 1 revenue = $378 million.

» *Cost calculations.* Ask yourself:

    – What will it take to secure/build the resources?

    – How much will each key activity cost?

    – How much will it cost to secure/reward the partners?

Now that you have worked out your revenue and identified your key costs you can calculate when you will break even with table 5b.1. Tally the totals for each period and compare costs to revenues and estimate profit. (This is a reality check for the viability of your innovation.)

Table 5b.1: viability assumption table

Cost items	MVP	Year 1	Year 2	Year 3
Product development	$	$	$	$
Marketing	$	$	$	$
Sales & distribution	$	$	$	$
Legal	$	$	$	$
Human resource	$	$	$	$
Partner fees	$	$	$	$
Total costs	$	$	$	$
Revenue	$	$	$	$
Total profits	$	$	$	$

TIPS

Sense check your estimates by asking yourself:

» Which costs don't come across as believable? Why?

» Which costs might be underbaked? What could you have missed?

» What alternative ideas do you have to reduce the costs?

Test the cost assumptions with someone outside the team— ideally a commercial professional. Seek feedback and ideas on how to make the cost assumptions robust and lean.

STEP 5: CAPTURE LEARNINGS

Following your tests you need to analyse the results to see if you've validated or invalidated your hypotheses and to identify key learnings. The more vivid and understandable your results, the more definitive they'll be for you and the more convincing they'll be for your stakeholders.

Start by synthesising your observations from the test using the following categories:

» *Likes.* What did customers like about the solution? Why?

» *Dislikes and improvements.* What did customers dislike about the solution and what improvements did they suggest? Why?

» *New questions to explore.* What new questions did the test prompt that you'd like to explore in the next iteration?

» *New hypotheses and ideas.* What new hypotheses and ideas did the test inspire that you'd like to develop and test in the next iteration?

Using these questions forces you to be structured and rigorous about capturing the learning from the testing.

TEST LEARNING BOARD

We then capture the outcome and validated learning of each test with the Test Learning Board (see figure 5b.8, overleaf).

The test learning feeds into the Learning Board. Keep in mind that the result is *what* happened and the learning is *why* it happened.

Idea name	**ON-DEMAND RIDE**
Experiment number and date	#3 — 28 March 2008
Hypothesis	We believe that people will drive strangers in their cars in return for payment
Target learning	To understand if there is a supply side to our solution
Test type	Quantitative survey
Result	Validated — 6% of suppliers tested said yes
Learning	People were comfortable driving strangers due to the security of passengers having accounts set up and the monitoring of the trip through their device and GPS
Decision	There is adequate supply for our solution — progress to next riskiest assumption.

Figure 5b.8: Test Learning Board

***

Once you have completed a test of your riskiest assumption you need to make an informed decision, based on your test learnings, on how to best proceed. Making a Progress/Pivot/Perish decision after each experiment is critical to ensure you are not wasting money and effort on dead ideas, features and projects. Success also includes walking away from projects that aren't going to fly.

ITERATE

The next step is to update your Business Model Canvas. Then you repeat the experimentation cycle:

1. identify the next riskiest assumption

2. experiment design

3. prototype

4. test

5. learn

6. progress/pivot/perish

7. canvas

You keep experimenting until you've validated and de-risked a desirable, feasible and viable solution and business model.

When you're running multiple experiments Steve Blank recommends using the Business Model Canvas as a weekly scorecard; it's a great way to track the changes to the business model based on the results of each experiment and output from your Test Learning Board.

TIP

Each time the Business Model Canvas is updated, take a photo to track the history of changes. Print the photos and put them beside the current business model (see figure 5b.9)

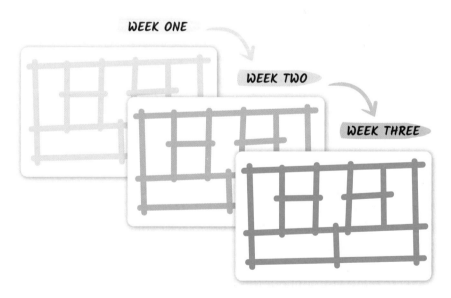

Figure 5b.9: updated business models

NEXT STEPS

At the end of this journey you'll have a short list of robust and desirable concepts (solutions) with de-risked business models that are feasible and viable, as well as some that have justifiably perished. It's also possible through your journey that you may have uncovered other opportunities that look ripe for further exploration in future projects.

The concepts that have evolved their way through this entire front-end of innovation process are now validated and ready for the business case. This makes it a lot easier to raise the money needed to complete the project. Following business case approval your concepts go into the back end of the innovation journey. You're not at the end yet, but importantly you have the confidence that you're backing the right solutions.

The steps following business case are:

» commitment to actually building the product, service or experience

» launching it.

Key activities will include:

» brand and design development

» product development

» launch plans

» launch.

The Idea Canvas and modified Business Model Canvas, plus other specific organisational and industry technical briefs, form the basis of briefing your winning concepts to your development and commercialisation teams. If you've followed this approach correctly these teams would have been represented in the cross-functional project team(s) throughout this journey. Also, a core of the front end of innovation team should flow right through to launch. This makes the remaining innovation stages far smoother and more likely to be successful, with ongoing shared ownership of the customer needs and insights and solutions. This is in contrast to the more traditional handover approach from one siloed department to another, where the integrity of the customer insight and the ideas can be lost through poor communication and collaboration and a lack of buy-in to the proposition.

You are now not only well on your way to launching a successful innovation, but on your way to building better-performing teams and innovation practices that can sustain these efforts, constantly innovating to create new value.

Learnings

- Once you have some solutions it is important you put them back in front of customers in the form of prototypes to get some feedback on desirability. Do they matter to the customer?

- Prototyping is about bringing your ideas to life to make them testable.

- Prototyping for desirability should be quick, cheap and low fidelity.

- Prototypes can be concept boards, storyboards, roleplays, physical objects and digital.

- Your first rounds of prototyping and testing are not about whether you can make it, but whether, if you made it, it would matter to the customer.

- Customer testing is a specialist skill best run by qualitative and quantitative researchers.

- Don't start translating your solution into a Business Model Canvas until you know it is desirable. Any sooner is a waste of time and effort.

- Evolve, validate and de-risk your business model by ideating, hypothesising and running experiments to prototype, test and learn.

- Identify ballpark costs and revenue before proceeding to business case.

Questions for innovators and leaders

- Does your organisation give the same amount of weighting to desirability as it does feasibility and viability? Where is your organisation's bias?

- Do you prioritise validating concepts with customers before going into commercial analysis?

- Do your innovation teams have access to prototyping tools for low- to high-fidelity prototypes and qualitative and quantitative researchers to run the test and learn steps?

- Are you open to challenge the business model for your new innovations to create more breakthrough and differentiated offerings?

- Are you promoting a culture of experimentation and allowing for some failures in order to learn and grow?

OVER TO YOU

— YOUR JOURNEY TO INNOVATION FLOW

I hope this book and the framework, processes, tools, mindsets and behaviours it shares will help you master the front end of innovation, so you and your teams can be more successful at innovation. Innovation for too long has had unnecessarily high rates of failure, because, according to Innovation Management expert Robert Cooper, typically we focus 90 per cent of our efforts and resources on the back end of innovation, not the front. Getting the front end of innovation right is the key to unlocking innovation success. Just like you wouldn't skip laying the foundations when building a house, you shouldn't skip laying the foundations for successful innovation. You might get to market faster, but with an inferior product that will fall over, and the rework to get it right will be hugely expensive and time consuming.

A REPEATABLE METHOD FOR INNOVATION SUCCESS

Using the full suite of customer-centric innovation and design methods such as Design Thinking, Business Model Canvas and Lean Startup in the right way, at the right time and in the right sequence (as shown in figure 7) will help you succeed in the front end of innovation.

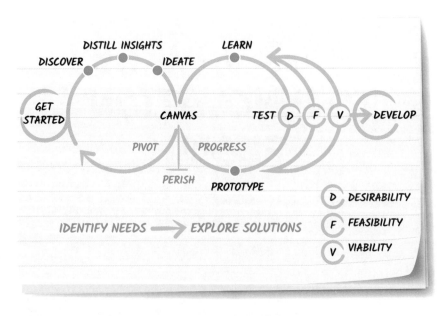

Figure 7: integrated design-led innovation

WHEN AND WHERE TO APPLY IT

Traditionally, the business world has often relied on deductive thinking, where there is only one right solution to a problem. This assumes that all of the relevant factors are self-evident and logically certain. While this may be the case sometimes, it is hardly ever the case for innovation, where you are creating something for the future where there is a lot of uncertainty. Design-led or customer-centric innovation helps you solve challenges where the root causes of a problem are not always known and there might be more than one right solution. When we are innovating we are open to there being more than one right solution. So you can probably deduce from this that, when you know the problem and know the solution, you do not require a design-led approach. In this case a design-led approach would be too elaborate.

You can use Innovation Triage (see figure 8, overleaf) to help you decide where to start your innovation journey. If you don't know the customer problems within your opportunity area then you need to start at the beginning of the process. If, however, you've already conducted some customer research in your opportunity area and have identified the customer problem, but not yet the solution, then start with stage 4: Ideate. And if you've already identified the problem and the solution, and you have problem-solution fit (a desirable concept), then you can start with the Business Model Canvas at stage 5: Experiment feasibility and viability. Lastly, if you know the solution, but don't know the problem, then either you have a technology looking for a problem or you're just jumping to the solution.

HOW LONG DOES IT TAKE?

There is no definitive rulebook on how long to spend on the front end of innovation. Many factors come into consideration. Most obviously, because you are creating something for the future that doesn't yet exist you can't know exactly how long it will take. However, given the evidence that quality up-front work in the front end of innovation will increase your chance of innovation success—and that most organisations spend too little effort and time here—you can probably rightly assume that your organisation could increase the time it allocates there.

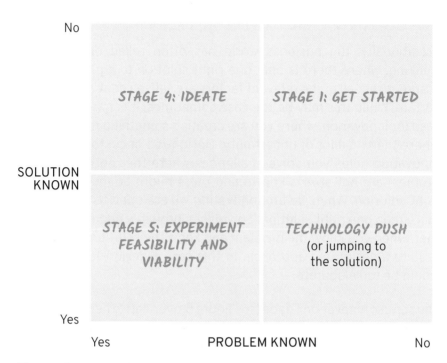

No

STAGE 4: IDEATE   STAGE 1: GET STARTED

SOLUTION
KNOWN

STAGE 5: EXPERIMENT   TECHNOLOGY PUSH
FEASIBILITY AND   (or jumping to
VIABILITY   the solution)

Yes

Yes   PROBLEM KNOWN   No

Figure 8: Innovation Triage

This is why I believe the trend towards five-day design sprints needs to be rethought, as it puts speed (and sometimes theatre) ahead of rigour and success. Why would anyone in their right mind want to shortcut the stages so critical to innovation success? Five-day sprints do have their time and place. From my experience they are better suited for incremental, minor redesign and usability type projects, not evolutionary to revolutionary innovation. A word of warning—beware of smoke and mirrors over rigour and delivering desirable, feasible and viable results. As Thomas Edison said, 'Innovation is 1% inspiration and 99% perspiration'.

How long it will take will be largely influenced by what type of innovation you are aiming to bring to market—your level of innovation ambition. For example, is it incremental, evolutionary or revolutionary innovation. Note that it is a worthy strategy to have a portfolio of projects covering each type of innovation. Here are ball park time frames for the different ranges of innovation:

» *Incremental:* If you're optimising existing products for existing customers (incremental innovation), it typically requires anything from five days to three months for the front end of innovation. This is the most suitable of the three ranges for a five-day design sprint. You still need to stay true to your customers' needs, though, otherwise you risk damaging an already successful brand and experience.

» *Evolutionary:* Innovating into new markets or new products typically takes longer than incremental innovation. Normally you'd spend three to six months in the front end of innovation for this kind of innovation.

» *Revolutionary:* Looking for that breakthrough innovation requires a larger effort. These projects can typically take a minimum of six months, which is why it's important to run with a mixed portfolio of innovation projects. You need to keep developing and maintaining what is working for you now while exploring new things for the organisation and market. No matter what level of innovation ambition or horizon we are aiming for, we often uncover ideas for the other two levels.

Don't stop using customer-centric innovation after launch. This methodology is equally applicable to optimise and evolve your products, services and experiences after launch. You'll find it useful in unlocking new insights and ideas for all marketing and business activities.

WHAT'S NEXT?

Your own journey doesn't stop once you become a practitioner of the front end of innovation. Mastery involves experimenting with new methods and leading others in their adoption and proficiency to run it. Once you feel like you've mastered the process and methods outlined in this book and had some successes, start experimenting with your own approaches. Identify the pain points in your own process, and look for new techniques to solve these and run experiments. And let me know how you go. Also, if you have any questions or want to use me as a sounding board then please reach out (you can find me on LinkedIn or email me at nathan@methodry.com).

Look for opportunities to take design-led innovation beyond your circle of influence. As you have successes you'll likely be asked by other teams to help, or be given bigger teams and projects to lead. Give back and share what you've learned.

Now ... get on your way and innovate!

About the author

Nathan Baird is an internationally experienced author, speaker and innovation consultant living in Sydney, Australia. He is one of the world's leading Design Thinking practitioners, having practiced and taught it since before it was called Design Thinking. He is the founder and managing director of customer-driven innovation and growth firm Methodry. He was previously a Partner of Design Thinking for global management consultancy KPMG, where he established and led KPMG's Human Centred Design practice, helping the firm and its clients create customer-centric innovation and transformation. He has run 100s of innovation projects, 1000s of workshops and spent tens of thousands of hours practicing and training innovation across most industries and continents with global giants and market-leading organisations like the Australian Institute of Sport, Bausch & Lomb, Commonwealth Bank of Australia, Diageo, Les Mills, Siemens and Unilever, as well as many small-medium enterprises, startups, not-for-profits and government.

He is super passionate about democratising innovation while balancing the need to maintain rigorous standards of teaching and practice to enable all individuals, teams, organisations and countries to prosper and flourish through design-led innovation.

In his 20 years of experience in business Nathan has worked both client side and consultancy side, as well as running his own company. When he is not helping organisations innovate he can be found on a road or mountain bike cycling out in the hills and the bush of the countryside, either with his family and/or with mates.

Index